# A POSH AFFAIR

# A POSH AFFAIR

## Sixty Years of The Posh

**Tony Broughton**

*To John*

*Tony Broughton*

# A Posh Affair

First Published in 2017 by FastPrint Publishing Peterborough, England.

Copyright © Tony Broughton, 2017

The moral right of Tony Broughton to be identified as the author of this work has been asserted by him in accordance with the Copyright, Designs and Patents Act 1988 and any subsequent amendments thereto.

All rights reserved. No part of this book may be reproduced in any form by photocopying or any electronic or mechanical means, including information storage or retrieval systems, without permission in writing from both the copyright owner and the publisher of the book.

A CIP catalogue record for this book is available from the British Library

Paperback ISBN 978-178456-495-7

Printed and bound in England by www.printondemand-worldwide.com

www.fast-print.net/bookshop

# Contents

1. Introduction
2. The Love Affair Begins
3. Non League No More
4. 1966 And All That
5. Double Edge Sword
6. Five Seasons In The Basement
7. Hail The Messiah
8. Breaking Up Is Hard To Do
9. Life After The Messiah
10. Division Four On The Horizon
11. Wiles Woes
12. Are The Good Times Back
13. The Devaney Years
14. Chris Turns It Round
15. A Season To Remember
16. In With The Big Boys
17. After The Lord Mayors Show
18. Still Hoping
19. Bazza Frys In
20. Nearly A Perfect Ten
21. A Wembley Return
22. Back To Reality
23. Same Old Story
24. Goulden Times Again
25. Back In The Basement Again
26. Wright Or Ron
27. The Money Man Arrives
28. Coming To Terms With Life
29. Heartbreak At The Palace
30. A Piece Of Silver Ware
31. The Underacieving Seasons.
32. On The Buses With Dot And Olive
33. How The Game Has Changed In Sixty Years
34. The Good The Bad And The Ugly
35. From London Road To The Abax
36. Posh People

# Introduction

About me Tony Broughton the author this is my sixtieth odd year of watching the Posh a life time of ups and downs. I think if I spoke the truth more downs than ups but one good thing is that since getting into the League we have remained in it, not like a lot of clubs since then now playing non league football or now defunct.

This book is dedicated to the memory of my daughter Sharon Anne Evans who passed away on the 31st March 2015 aged 41 years old after a long illness who is dearly missed by myself my wife Anne and her lovely little dog Lady Pip and have written this as a tribute to her like me travelled all over the country watching our beloved Posh.

Over the last twenty years or perhaps more I have had lots of roles at the club mostly voluntary including working on the pitch, ground tours, chief steward on the away travel for many seasons, Junior Posh and now things have turned full circle now back on the Forever Posh Committee and helping with Junior Posh. Since retiring have taken on the role as Group Co bringing in local teams to do flag bearing and penalties at half time including ground tours against Peter Burrow and PB our mascots this is highly popular and completely full season by Christmas and brought in much needed funds for the club and have a refurbished room thanks to Forever Posh under the Main Stand.

In April 2015 only about a couple of weeks after Sharon Anne passing away I was called in to see our Chief Executive Bob Symms who asked how me and my wife Anne were coping then asked if we felt able to go with a party of staff to Football Association Dinner and Awards in London as the club had elected me as the Club Hero I was so upset and in floods of tears as Sharon Anne bless her would have been so proud of me as I was to be nominated although did not win the main trophy but was so pleased that it went to Brian Murphy the kit man at Birmingham City he had lost two of his children too think it was cancer and now was now not well enough to travel to the awards when things happen and you feel sorry for yourself their always someone worse off Brian sadly lost his fight with cancer in the July 2015. All the nominations received a glass plaque with name and club engraved on it and it sits proudly on the wall unit next to Sharon Anne's pictures.

The book the A POSH AFFAIR is not a complete history of the club as brilliantly wrote by Mick Robinson and Andy Groom as I don't profess to watching every game in sixty years far from it had to work on Saturdays after leaving school, then playing Peterborough League football for a few seasons and missing out on most away games in our last spell in the Championship as Sharon was so ill and I wanted to be near to home. The book is about the comings and goings in those seasons the games that left a memory for me and over view of the seasons, trips on the Away Travel, People who over the years I have met at the Posh, how the game has changed over the 60 years and players who have impressed me and the ones who have been a waste of money and how London Road now the Abax has changed. The book has been written mostly from memory with little research sorry Mick and Andy did refer to yours more than a few times. Happy reading tried to make it humorous hope I don't upset to many people and my memory has served me well. Tony

**THE LOVE AFFAIR BEGINS**

Have to blame my father Wally Broughton who got me started watching my beloved club he like me supported them for fifty odd years mostly at home and the big cup games away if he could afford it after settling in a new job at London Brick Company after the Second World War which saw him go with one of the D-day back up armies and across Europe to Germany. He said he did not want to go and was glad to get home and was not at all upset when I buried all his medals in our garden in Orchard Street in New Fletton where you could nearly see the floodlights when they were erected.

My early memories of Posh games were going to watch the Reserves in the Eastern Counties League they got such big gates. Some of the names can remember in the stiffs or Reserves were Adam Dickson in goal with his roll neck jersey, Bobby Middlemas, Des Farrow, Cliff Sansby and Jimmy Longworth who I still see most mornings in our local newsagents in Fletton and must have also included Peter McNamee who told me recently when I met him he had three seasons in the Reserves before breaking into the first team and said did I remember Tessie Balogun playing he was the first coloured player to play for the club in 1957 he said he would never get in the bath with the lads when he dropped his towel one day the lads could see why he asked Peter to get him a women he declined. I would have to wait a big longer to watch such stars as Freddie Martin, George Hair, Andy Donaldson, Paddy Sloan, Jim Kelly and Dougie Taft and co.

One my earliest memories are of the first team games is waiting outside not at a game but in front of Dobson's Decorating shop next to the Peacock on London Road along with a lot of fans outside the Players entrance as referee Mr Husband awarding Lincoln City a disputed penalty in the last minute of the game in front of a record crowd of over 22,000. Think the culprit was full back Ray Barr who lodged in London Road. The replay at Sincil Bank produced another thriller going to extra time with Posh winning in extra time 5-4 after a draw 2-2 in normal time an Andy Donaldson hat trick plus goals from Ray Smith and Dennis Emery to get the Posh a plum draw with First Division Huddersfield Town at Leeds Road in the Fourth Round and prompted a mass exodus from the city. I was overjoyed when Dad asked me would I like to go and off we went with over 10,000 odd fans on one of the special football train s from the London Brick think we left at about 7am in the morning saw my mates dad Stan Bell delivering the milk on his horse and cart usually under the covers at this time wishing we had heating to stop the bedroom windows freezing up. For the game Dad had made up a mascot for me one of my sisters dolls was beheaded he made a top hat complete with monocle and a board with up the Posh on it on the long journey with many of are we there yet from me. The Evening Telegraph printed thousands of UP THE POSH stickers that adorned the train carriage windows and anything that was static including a Policeman's helmet try doing that in today's game. The game was played in front nearly 49,000 but Posh although battling bravely were no match for the Terriers going down 3-1 in their team was a bandy legged youngster Dennis Law who was in our local paper before the game wearing NHS glasses what a great player he went on to be.

After this my parents said I could go to the First team games and now saw me going to the ground every Saturday with Reserves at home if the first team away. Now playing football at school myself and in the team at St.Augustines still have team photo with all the other lads in tie up collars and me in my red v necked shirt my idol was Duncan Edwards as I played left half and cried for days when he was killed in the Munich Air Crash along with so many other great players who I had seen earlier in the first Cup Final on television had seen at one of my Granddads neighbours in Elm Street Fletton lose to Aston Villa the Villa team including keeper Nigel Simms and winger Peter McParland who were to join us well by their sell by date a few seasons later. Watched the Posh pick up the Midland League title for the second time rattling in 148 goals past bemused keepers often toying with opponents with the big crowds shouting shoot. Dennis Emery netting 43 league goals which surely will not be beaten but as you will read further it was but in the Football League.

The 57/58 season Posh won the Midland League again for the third time me seeing all the home games again heavy beatings were the norm and London Road was a fortress poor old Denaby United returned on a 9-0 trashing and Doncaster Rovers Res, Bradford City Reserves and Corby Town did not fare any better losing 8-2, 7-0 and 8-1 respectively. Posh now more than ever were wanting to get into the Football League as the League Res sides were now leaving the Midland League and going into the Football Combination again they were not successful and after looking at another option decided to stay in the Midland League 57/58 at least for the time being.

Posh were now putting in all the stops to get into the League with the erection of floodlights in mid season hosting the mighty Arsenal in a friendly to open them and other games against Division 1 sides but again at the end of the season they fell short in the voting for election despite appointing the strict Jimmy Hagan as manager and winning a now depleted league and again having a good FA Cup run 16,000 of us saw us see of Headington United now Oxford United at London Road then off on another away day special being drawn away to high flying Fulham from Division Two could just about see over high fence to see the likes of stars like Tony Macedo one of my favourite keepers at the time, Johnny Haynes, George Cohen, Jimmy the Chin Hill, Tosh Chamberlin and Graham Leggett are names I still remember again the Posh had another 10,000 following the game finished goalless the replay in front of 21,600 at London Road saw the Cottagers go through with a single goal victory.

Back to an ever smaller Midland League in 1959/60 but big things are on the horizon after cruising to the top of the league even a great FA Cup run could stop us gaining our fifth title win. After beating Bury Town yes in the Fourth Qualifying round those days 7-1 in front of nearly 10,000 we saw off two Football League teams Shrewsbury at home and Walsall away which paired us away to Second Division Ipswich Town a game that never should have been played as it snowed on the train journey and the pitch was covered in carpet of snow but the Posh gained their biggest Cup Giant Killing upset in the club's history so far. After the Tractor Boys scoring first but wing half Jim Rayner levelled things up before the break but not before full back Jim Walker was injured just in front of us and although trainer Johnny Anderson got him able to carry on only as a passenger on the wing no substitutes in those days. Again the hosts went back into the lead before Golden Boy Dennis Emery levelled and when netting the winner in the dying embers of the game to beat the Tractor Boys and the snow this was the last time they were to lose to non league opposition until Lincoln City beat them this season. At the time hailed as one of the clubs best performances but ever better times were to come despite after a grand display against Sheffield Wednesday losing 2-0 with goals in the last quarter of the match.

Posh had the honour of winning the Sunday Pictorial Giant Killers Cup wonder if we were allowed to keep it now is hidden away somewhere in the stadium. Can remember writing to Stratton Smith the Sports Editor about our exploits and he sent me a team photo graph the same that appeared in the paper was so chuffed it hung it my bedroom for years. This was the last season of non league football at again they finished top of the pile in the Midland League but much greater things were to come.

## NON LEAGUE NO MORE

Posh were finally elected to the Football League on 28th May 1960 the writing was on the wall Posh could not be ignored any more finishing behind Oldham by four votes one in front of Hartlepool's and six in front of Southport with Gateshead being banished to non league football. The irony of the teams elected was the first letter of each team spelt POSH overall justice had been done after 21 attempts to be elected.

We now prepared for our first season in the Fourth Division which kicked off at home to Wrexham manager Jimmy Hagan bringing in eight new players and now us lads had different names to emulate when we played in our local Fletton Recreation Ground till it got dark and even then played under the lights from Marshalls garage until the plastic Wembley plastic balls got a puncture and we had to repair it with a hot poker nobody could afford a proper ball if they did they were our heroes even though they were crap at the game.

When the Bridge Fair was on we used to have battle royal games against the Fair Kids but it was never Fair because they wore hobnailed boots and we only had plimsolls or if you were lucky baseball boots. In the summer we switched to cricket but the Fair Kids were never clever enough to play that, for our make believe Test Matches we obtained a push mower and mowed a wicket and had all the equipment bats, pads and gloves this we played until the start of the footy season or till we got fed up with Roy Killingworth batting for hours think he was taught by Geoffrey Boycott certainly as slow scoring as him.

Over 17,000 flocked to London Road to see us beat Wrexham in the first league game 3-0 with goals from Dennis Emery, Peter McNamee and Terry Bly which was the start of a record scoring season for him. Most of my games this season were at home as Mum and Dad bringing up a young family could not afford for me and dad to go away and sometimes he used to work overtime on match days for the extra money.

The games that stick in my mind that season are the 4-1 win against Crystal Palace at home over 21,000 fans seeing Terry Bly net the first of his seven hat tricks that season and winger Billy Hails who used to live in one of the clubs houses near the Glebe Road entrance for years Billy sadly passed away this season as I write and being inducted into The Posh Hall of Fame a month after with his son Julian receiving his accolade.

Another one is the 6-2 mauling of Doncaster Rovers perhaps because I had to go to Boys Brigade instead was not impressed was so scared to play truant from it someone would have spilt the beans especially as the Captain lived down our street. The best game of this season was the local derby against the Cobblers nearly 23,000 packing the ground with both teams vying for the top spot Posh being a point clear. The day quickly sour for us Cobblers running up a 3-0 lead but an early goal by Peter Namee which he added to on the hour and then Dennis Emery goal earned us a draw this was the first local derby and certainly one I remembered with no prisoners taken by either side.

In the FA the club was to have another epic run with early round wins against Dover and Torquay United then another away trek to Second Division Portsmouth winning 2-1 with goals from half back Keith Ripley whose car used be forever parked outside the Orchard Street Library he must have been a book worm or something like that, Jim Walkers car also used to be parked down our street but that was coacher he was courting his wife to be. Billy Hails netting the other goal and earning a money spinner against First Division Aston Villa in the Fourth Round.

A game that proved a nightmare for centre half Roy Banham who was playing because Norman Rigby was out injured can see him now laying on his stomach in the mud as he headed under pressure from Gerry Hitchin's into his own net to give the Villa the lead in front of 28,000 fans a record crowd up to that date still rib him about it when he visits the ground ask him has he brought his compass. Billy Hails came up with the posh leveller to send Posh to Villa Park on the next Tuesday no cooling off period in those days for television coverage, stewarding and Police cover. Because it was a school day I had to listen to the game on the radio which was a change from listening to Radio Luxemburg and the likes of Gunsmoke etc. Again another big exodus to Villa Park and lots of our supporters never got in the gates locked at 64,500. The run came to an end with the Posh going down 2-1 our goal being scored by Peter McNamee and it was back to the bread and butter of Division Four as promotion was within our grasp and a great run of games saw us promoted with seven games to go the players who upset our run was centre forward George Hudson of Accrington Stanley who netted a hat trick a few seasons later he was a star at London Road.

Posh won the championship with a 3-3 draw at Southport and saw us clock up 134 goals in the league centre forward Terry Bly netting 52 including seven hat tricks followed by Ray Smith who netted 17, nimble winger Peter McNamee 16 and golden boy Dennis Emery 15 but I am sure in today's game he would have the most assists we used to can them passes in those days.

Len Shipman of The Football Association presented the trophy to the Posh he was to be very instrumental in the demise of the club later in this era as you read on. For the next season1961/2 manager Jimmy Hagan relied on the same players who were so successful but brought in Ollie Hopkins from Barnsley a strong centre half who eventually replaced Norman Rigby he was soon a favourite with his fearsome tackles in one game on a mud bound surface his slide tackle saw him crash into the Main Stand Enclosure wall we all expected him to go off on stretcher but all he did was dust himself down and carried on playing.

The next season saw another eventful one perhaps the stand out games were beating Watford home and away at London Road in front of 18,000 fans when followed weeks later with the lowest gate so far a mere 12,500 witnessed the trashing of Brentford. New signing centre forward George Hudson joined from Accrington Stanley and despite netting twice at Crystal Palace was unable to stop a 5-2 defeat nearly 29,000 packing Selhurst Park, he was to go on net 16 times that season but along way behind Terry Bly with 29 goals.

We were on another FA run beating Colchester after three games the last one taking place at the neutral Norwich City stadium. The 3-0 win was tinged with sadness as the clubs golden boy Dennis Emery was involved in an accident with a lorry to pick up the team coach from the ground the injury finished his career playing a further three games the next season before moving to Bedford due to overtaking on a wet road cost him a great future in the game a sad loss to the club his 22 games in the season he had already netted 15 times.

The cup exploits continued with the long haul to Torquay United winning 4-1 then the mighty Posh took another big scalp beating Newcastle United at St.James Park I being in the 3,000 odd fans that made the journey lady luck had a bit to play with the host having a goal chalked off for offside before Terry Bly netted to send us Posh fans home in raptures. But all good things come to an end and in the Fourth Round Sheffield United ended our hopes in front of 28,000 fans to coast into a three goal lead after just twenty minutes before George Hudson netted a consolation goal for the Posh.

Even a four match winning streak at the end of the season could only give them a fifth place slot which in these days would have given us a playoff position and netting 107 league goals.

The next season 1962/3 manager Jimmy Hagan shocked the fans before the season started with selling Terry Bly for £10,000 to Coventry City in his two seasons he had netted 81 goals in 88 games for us and also Granite Head Norman Rigby was given a free to Boston United after 11 seasons at the club and were both have been inducted into our Hall of Fame in the reception at the Abax and the popular keeper Jack Walls moved on to Kings Lynn the 1960-1 team was breaking up. His replacement Dick Beattie a Scottish u23 international I can always remember him passing me in his swish sports car when I waiting for the bus to take us to school at Orton no more sickies which I made miraculous recovery when I heard the school bell ring he going by on route to the ground for training his car could this have been bought from his games he threw one of game being letting in a soft goal against QPR at London Road which Posh lost 2-1 with his helping hand for the visitors.

Despite being 2nd in the table posh fans were shocked with the news that Jimmy Hagan had been sacked supposedly on the spot. More departures saw other members of our championship side of 1960/1 side move on Billy Hails who joined Tommy Robson at the Cobblers and blonde haired inside forward Ray Smith also joined him after being at the club since 1956 recently installed into the Posh Hall of Fame.

The new manager was former goalkeeper George Fairbrother and on his second spell as manager one of first unpleasant dealings for him was the clubs fall out with the Evening Telegraph due to a game that was played against a watching Cambridge United team after our game at London Road was called off and both teams played against each other but I have a memory of the game being played in Fletton Recreation ground but could be wrong, I'm sure someone will correct me. This led to a dispute with the club and the press and caused Posh to launch The Posh Post which I am sure fans have still got in their attics with old posh programmes.

The big freeze saw the team have a break from Boxing Day till the middle of February but it did not stop us youngsters playing games in the local Fletton Recreation Ground with now getting older we went from last picks for the teams to first pick and sometimes captains I became first pick because I played in goal and went home with the aroma of dog muck on my hands and now wearing a track suit top that new signing Alan Morton a local lad who lived with his parents in Fletton who had been released by the mighty Arsenal told all my mates it was an Arsenal top but thing it was a Kings School one really.

Posh eventually went out of the FA cup in the Third Round a game that played in the middle of February now we look at that round taking place around the first week end in January after beating Nott's County and beating non league Enfield in front of nearly 17,000 fans at London Road eventually losing to Derby County at the old Baseball Ground how has the FA Cup been devalued gates in the Second Round replays as I write this attendances for some league teams down to less than 2,000 fans with perhaps reduced admission prices being charged by clubs.

Another big loss during the season was the transfer of Terry Bly to Coventry followed later in the by season George Hudson to The Sky Blues. The match that springs to my mind is the 3-3 draw at High field Road Coventry after being 3-0 down at half time on a bitterly cold day just after Christmas with two goals from inside forward Ray Horobin and one of my favourites at the time Tony Moulden.

This was a season of changing fortunes and to make things worse we finished the season in sixth place now a playoff spot to champions the Cobblers eleven points adrift despite having a squad of 27 players bit like today's squads but we ran two senior teams and substitutes were a thing of the now near future. The next season I started to make my first million and fifty-five years on still waiting when I started work as a Junior Carpet Salesman for Fairways in Broadway which meant that I had to work Saturdays think my wage was top line three pounds and fifteen shillings and my love affair was now down to dates in mid week or the occasional game on a Saturday I left home for work phoned up to say I was sick and wander about town to kick off time hoping that you did not bump into anybody who would spill the beans from work or people who knew my parents. I used to hate seeing all the fans streaming by the windows to watch my beloved Posh, big deal we had half day closing on Thursday afternoon that was spend having chunks kicked out of me in the Thursday League playing for Peterborough Wanderers by the likes of Peterborough Police etc. Posh made some good signings one of the best being Derek Dougan from Aston Villa along with Willie Duff a keeper from Scottish Football but a good one and the hard Frank Rankmore from Cardiff City they were to be responsible in the clubs epic run this season. Sadly the club released Dennis Emery after 8 seasons he never recovered his former form after his accident The club were not such a force in 1963/4 season with only Jim Walker, Peter McNamee and squad player Ellis

Stafford remaining from the 1960/1 championship team. After a bad run of defeats and not finding the net the axe fell on manager George Fairbrother no different to the game today the new manager was Gordon Clark from Sheffield Wednesday appointed just before the end of the campaign which was the Posh finish in 10th place our lowest finish so far in the league despite Derek Dougan netting twenty goals and beating Champions Coventry City 2-0 at the end of the season remember standing in the packed Moy's Lane no segregation in those days Derek Dougan and Peter Thompson netting in front 26,000 fans the biggest attendance for a league game at London Road.

The epic FA Cup run of 1964/5 started with beating non league Salisbury again in front of 10,000 at London Road then defeating QPR in a replay at home which I was able to see as a night game pint size Peter Deakin who still lives in the city and was recently inducted into the club Hall of Fame scored both goals then a Doog the nickname of Derek Dougan hat trick saw off Chesterfield. The Third Round draw we paired at home to the mighty Arsenal and I would be working. As so many fans would be watching the game and also was the day of Winston Churchill's funeral being shown live on television Mr Spinks the owner said I could have the afternoon off and go to the game bless him. What an afternoon that turned out to be 30,056 which was then a record attendance at London Road I watched from the terracing on the Glebe Road side the Gunners playing a full strength side not like top clubs today with squad players in the FA cup. They took the lead just before the break through John Radford the unbelievable happened when Derek Dougan netted the leveller on 72 minutes but better things to come as winger Peter McNamee netted at the Moy's Lane end four minutes from time despite the Gunners throwing everything at us can't remember if they sent the keeper up in those days like today.

The Posh held on in joyous scenes and can still see the Gunners players sinking to their knees. What a great day for the city will always remember Winston Churchill's funeral as the day we beat the Gunners. In the league we hovered just about mid table with all my visits now only on evening games or the odd Saturday holiday which was hard to get off as a busy day for business.

The fifth round paired us away at home to then Second Division Swansea Town again Mr Spink of Fairways looked after me well with another afternoon off but the game was not as eventful perhaps the one thing I can remember was the Swans dirty tactics as the previous round neither side managing to find the net but the ground record was beaten again 30,096 packed London Road sure lots of supporters went home with wet patches on their trousers as we were packed like sardines on the Glebe Road terracing and going to the toilet was impossible. The replay held three days later saw the Posh win 2-0 again in front of nearly 30,000 fans at Vetch Field with two goals from little Peter Deakin and little Peterborough United were in the Quarter Final of the FA cup and drawn away at Stamford Bridge to the mighty Chelsea and a mass exodus followed them to the game but sadly without me my luck had run out I had to work I was gutted no good playing truant as they knew where I would be. One young lady at the store was determined to go despite what the management had said but when the Evening Telegraph came out on the Monday she was in a picture of a group of fans on the front page on Peterborough North Station poor old Wendy Beeby joined the unemployed on Tuesday morning. They say the Camera Never Lies how true. The game was over before it started Bert Murray the Chelsea full back who later was going to star in the 1973/4 Fourth Division Championship side for us and still lives locally as one of his tackles he had a good teacher at the Bridge in Chopper Ron Harris ended ginger haired captain Vic Crowes game although he came back as a passenger think substitutes came in the next season and he scored our consolation goal.

The host ran into a four goal lead before this and went on to add another in the last minute in front of nearly 64,000 fans so it was a successful day money wise for the club but ended our epic run. One of the things that I was not to see was my hero The Cat Peter Bonetti play in goal for Chelsea but at least I still did have a job to go to on Monday morning. Quite rightly the Posh were awarded the Sunday Mirror Giant Killers Cup wonder where that is now or did we have to give it back for the next seasons winners. Or if Peter McNamee has still got his watch from his testimonial game at the end of the season will ask him next time I see him. Despite a good run of results at the close of the season the posh finished 8th in the table?

**1966 AND ALL THAT**

The 1965/6 season was highlighted by England winning the World Cup before goal line technology linesman Tariq Bahramov from Azerbaijan becoming a hero for our players and back in his country a Football stadium being named after him I was lucky enough to get tickets for some of the England group matches and the only game played at the White City Stadium France v Uruguay but again the season only brought joy for Posh fans in the Cup this time in the League Cup. Close season saw the popular Derek Dougan being transferred to Leicester City for £25,000 netting every two games on average in his career at London Road he was to be a big loss for the club but finances were not good and the club needed the money gates now down to the 7,000 mark and long standing Chairman Tommy Peake who had the Post Office in Gladstone Street was voted off the board of directors. The season was sparked by the League Cup victory at St.James Park beating Newcastle United with Mike Beasley further goals from Ollie Conmy and pint sized winger saw the club through to a 3-2 win to gain us a tie against Charlton and what a game it was Posh running out winners after being down 2-3 at the break the lads turned the game round and finished 4-3 winners with new goal scoring hero Johnny Byrne netting a hat trick to go with a first minute goal from Peter Deakin Byrne going on to net 25 goals in the season. Byrne repeated his hat trick in the next round of the League away to Millwall 4-1 with Peter Deakin completing the scorers and now we were given a home draw in the Fifth round against Burnley who were leaders of the First Division it was a game I was not allowed to go to as been off work and my parents would not let me go try doing that in today's world although did take in out on the landing wall and took a chunk out with a temper kick and trying to say it was an accident.

John Fairbrother not a popular choice with the fans scored two goals, Ollie Conmy and an owl goal giving the Posh a 4-0 win in front of nearly 15,000 fans but sadly I was not among them. Now in the Semi Finals but victory over the two legged games would not take us to Wembley that did not come in to the next season the draw matched us against W.B.A the first leg being away at the Hawthorne's can remember standing with hundreds outside the Evening Telegraph offices then in Broadway where the updates on the game come through we were in raptures when the young lady put up that Vic Crowe had scored early for us but before half time she was not so popular when Tony Brown levelled the scores very quickly and Graham Lovett put the Baggies into a 2-1 lead to take to London Road. The progress was now over shadowing our league form lying mid table and in between the legs the club went out of the FA Cup to Shrewsbury Town. The second leg saw over 18,000 see the Posh finish losing in all departments to a slick W.B.A team who ran into a 3-0 lead and despite Ollie Conmy and a late goal from centre half Frank Rankmore ran out winners with Tony Brown claiming a hat trick. After this the gates were in demise and posh finished 13th the lowest position since coming into the League. Late in the season Tony Millington the Welsh International signed for the club from Crystal Palace who proved to be a very popular signing and added to his Welsh caps in his Posh career.

## DOUBLE EDGED SWORD

Perhaps the worst season in the clubs short league history on the field and off it after a promising start and going out of the League Cup early to the Cobblers and not repeating our success of the last season we continued to fall down the league. The FA Cup brought us some relief despite but only spelt disaster to the club the next season. After beating Hereford United at home and Colchester United away in the third round we travelled to local non league Bedford Town with former Posh Golden Boy Dennis Emery in their team Posh running out winners 6-2 with nimble winger Tommy Watson bagging a hat trick in front of over 14,000 fans at the Eyrie the Eagles being a good Giant Killers themselves reaching the fourth round the season before going out to Everton in front of 18,000 now the capacity is down to just over 3,000 how times have changed. In the fourth Round we were away to Sunderland a game that was going to spell disaster to the club on two fronts the club being mauled 7-1 at Roker Park but lots worst to come.

After a good start to the 1967/8 campaign a couple of weeks after Bonfire night the Posh were to receive a rocket which rocked the club and us supporters as we were to be relegated back to Division Four at the end of the term for a number of off irregularities on the board who dished the punishment on the club was Mr Len Shipman who was later to present the Fourth Division Championship to us at our 1973/4 success needless to say he did not get a warm reception. Much bigger teams have got away with rule flouting and did not receive the penalty handed out to us and now if the clubs go into administration most have not paid the tax man all they receive is a point's deduction. Previous to this manager Gordon Clark I am sure guessed the fate of us and Rigger Norman Rigby the hard centre half and skipper from the 1960/1 championship side took over now to guide the team through the season and to an unfair demotion. Fans continued to back the side beating the Saddlers of Walsall who were top of the pile next game around now a young John Wile was in the team who was to join the club as manager at the end of his career he was a popular player who I thought should have played for England but his management skill was something very different.

As the season progressed the gates began eventually to fall to the 5,000 mark but again we had a run in the FA Cup after beating Falmouth and Margate both non league then we drew Portsmouth at home again I working Saturdays my new boss was not incommoding as my previous boss but was shocked when my girlfriend at the time and her friends come into the shop afterwards and see told me she ran on the pitch when Stuart Brace missed on the goal line at Posh lost to a lone Pompey goal. The season fizzled out for the club finishing just under half way perhaps the highlight was Colin Garwood netting a hat trick a hat trick in a end of season game beating the Cobblers 4-0 and at least we finished higher than them and we were playing basically friend lies after the judgement served on us. So now back to the Fourth division and it was going to be a few seasons until we returned to the Third what a time to change my job now at Freemans Mail Order and enjoyed 26 happy years working at a great company and for my sins met the Mrs Anne their and still together after have to think 45 years of her roasts and she has had to put up with allot of Posh suffering over that time.

**FIVE SEASONS IN THE BASEMENT**

At the start of the season 1968/9 Posh recorded a gate of over 8,000 for the first game against Exeter City but suddenly the fans realised they were watching basement football and the next league game it was down by over 2,000 fans. One good thing about the season was the signing of my mate Tommy Henry Robson from Newcastle United for £12,000 bet he found it different running out of the tunnel at London Road instead of being sucked out with the noise of the crowds at St. James Park what a signing he turned out to be. Think the fans could see us bouncing back first time that was not to be for another few seasons.

By the end of the year we were lying well under half way and that was not going to improve despite Norman Rigby resigning ending his long service with the club just after mid season to be known to our fans as a no nonsense defender a great leader but perhaps managing was not his cup of tea. At least the season did see another good run in the League Cup after overcoming Doncaster Rovers in the First Round after a replay a Jim Hall hat trick and a goal from little Peter Thompson saw us go through 4-2 and set us up for a night to remember being drawn at home to holders W.B.A us seeking our revenge for a couple of seasons ago. Over 16,000 fans flocked to London Road and we duly did it pint sized Peter Price who went on to earn Welsh International u23 caps while at the club opened the scoring added to by Peter Thompson Tony Brown pulled one back for the Baggies but the Posh held on and with the pitch invasion you would have thought we had won the cup.

The city was now buzzing again and thousands of us made the journey to the Fourth Round game against Tottenham Hotspurs at White Hart Lane against a full strength side not as the big boys do today with squad sides against lesser opponents. Remember this game for several reasons first Jimmy Greaves scoring with his head as rare as a Tommy Robson header the referee chalking off a Peter Thompson goal then the same player missing a sitter and the Posh losing to an odd goal. Worse was to come for me as the girl of my dreams gave me a dear John and was broken hearted on both fronts. Jimmy Iley was the man who took over from Norman Rigby we took over as player manager now in the twilight of his playing years having served Newcastle United and Tottenham Hotspur. He could not turn things around and at the end of the season we finished 18th the lowest finish so far the lowest game under 4,000 I was on the lookout for a new girlfriend and found the Mrs, and Jim Hall netted 20 times. Iley was not a man to delegate things he took everything corners from both sides running round the back of the goal, free kicks and throw ins despite his age the only thing he didn't take where penalties they were taken and mostly scored by Ollie Conmy.

The rest of his first season saw us go seven games without a loss but the favourites after our demotion finished up looking at the wrong end of Division Four. The season of 1968/9 saw one of favourite keepers Tony Millington being sold to Swansea then finishing his career at Wrexham after his retirement had a road accident that put him in a wheelchair and often used to stop and have a chat about the time he spent at the Posh when we visited the Racecourse Ground a lovely man no longer with us. A young centre half called Chris Turner joined the full time ranks what a career in the game he was to embark on he was joined by winger Bobby Moss from Fulham.

About now my short career in the Peterborough and District Football League was starting along with the Sunday Combination Morning League and Sunday League in the afternoon yes three games in a week end actually once played four when my Sunday League West Town United had a double header with First team and Reserves at home with me the only fit keeper. So again it was back to night games but with kick off times then 3-15 at London Road managed to get most second halves in if I was playing local firstly for Freemans, Lord Westwood then on to G.P.O. after saving two penalties in a game against their Reserve team at Itter Park and was snapped up by player/manager Geoff Manning who passed away recently perhaps one of the best players ever I played with and a great manager to be part of the Minor Cup winning team I think it was 1970/1 season and I think we also won promotion to Division Two but could be wrong it's a very long while ago.

Memories of this team came back very recently at dear old Derek Poole's funeral as the driver of the hearse was Mel Sambells who played on the wing in the team had not seen him since those days. Can remember being flattened by one of the aptly named Buddle brothers at Chatteris Engineers in the closing minutes of a game and being pealed out of the mud twenty stone into ten stone was not a fair match and being intimidated by tough centre forwards like Darrell Collins if I kick you I don't mean it at Ramsey SM. But did get one chance at the big time after getting married had a season at New England in the dizzy heights of Division One as Reserve keeper and got the call as Mick Cross was injured like Steve Zenchuk at Posh many years later when David Seaman got injured in the warm up but did better than him we beat Perkins 5-0.

How many newlywed wives would let their new husband play the day after getting married the day before today them are away on a exotic honey moon mine was spend keeping a clean sheet for West Town United at Longthorpe had the luxury of our own house which we still live in today. Jim Iley got one claim to fame at the Posh being the first Posh player to be sent off since we had got into the Football League his first time ever in his long career. After a poor start to the 69/70 season falling down to just above the relegation or was it still re-election still then but a great run of results with goals a plenty the best being the demolition of Oldham Athletic at London Road to the tune of 8-1 with Jim Hall netting four Peter Price a hat trick and Bobby Moss completing the rout.

I Was in London Road with Anne and thought that had converted her to football but she soon found out this was a one off and now forty years on has not got a clue about the game hence we have Sky in both downstairs rooms she is an expert on the cooking programmes. The turn of the year saw us in seventh place have another good cup run this time going out in Round Four after beating Luton Town in Round One, disposing of non league Falmouth Town in the Second Round at London Road then Plymouth Argyle made the long pilgrimage to the city and it was a long way home for them Posh recorded a 2-0 win. Round Four and a trip to Rotherham United at Millmoor and a lone Jim Hall goal put us through to Round Four to a trip to Gillingham missing out on another big club the Gills being then in Division Three was going to be a day to forget for us away fans going home with a 5-1 defeat with the manager Iley not a popular figure.

We did have a better end to the campaign and the average gate for the season was just over 6,000 not bad as we now only get that for the occasional game now of the 77 league goals we scored 54 were scored by three players big Jim Hall with 24, Peter Price 17 and Tommy Robson with13. The early seventies brought new industry to the city which lots of people moving from London to new homes in the city with firstly Westwood being built followed later by Ravensthorpe and Bretton the club hoped that these people would become a welcome influx of support as the they could not afford to pay the players summer wages and were bailed out by Supporters Club at the start of the 1970/1 season again this was not a season of much success not helped by the transfer of John Wile to W.B.A to serve a long successful career with them one of the best centre halves for the club up alongside the likes of Norman Rigby, Frank Rankmore and Chris Turner. All season we hardly got into the top half of the table. We went out of the F.A. Cup to then non league team Wigan Athletic at the old grim Springfield Park stadium where you did not walk to the toilet you aqua plainer down a muddy bank into them and don't think the stand windows had been cleaned since it had been built. But at least we got a bit of prize money don't know if they paid that to clubs in those days as we beat then Southern League opponents Wimbledon in Round One. Even Cambridge United where in the League now and managed to take then three points off us and late Peter Price goal at the Abbey gave us a point and then later in the season we lost 3-2 at London Road with old pals Jim Hall and Tommy Robson netting.

The club finished the season in 16th position and despite all the new families arriving in the city gates fell again to an average of just under 4,000 the mid November game saw an attendance of fewer than 3,000 against Darlington. Best signing this season was the capture of Arsenal Reserve team captain Jolly Jack Carmichael but he must thought had he made the wrong decision when we got a 6-0 pasting from Nott's County not long after he had joined our digest defeat in the league so far. It did not deter him going on to make 394 appearances for the club and rubbing shoulders with some of the World's greatest players in America at the end of his playing days at Posh and now has recently moved to live in the states. After a good start to the 1971/2 season followed by one win in six games we thought things were on the up with a 7-0 demolition of Barrow by the time I got to the game after playing on the Grange with 2pm kick off after playing we were 5-0 up the Posh scorers were hat tricks for Jim Hall and Peter Price and Ollie Conmy. By the time of the FA Cup came round we were well in the bottom half of the Division and needed two attempts to get by non league Redditch United trashing them at London Road 6-0 with two goals each from Jim Hall and Richie Barker and goals from Tommy Robson and Peter Price completing the scoring.

The next round was an easier passage again against non league opponents Enfield we recorded a 4-0 victory with Peter Price and Jim Hall recording a brace each. The next home game on New Year's Day we had a bumper holiday crowd of over 7,000 for the visit of Brentford the game ending 2-2. The Third Round saw the Tractor Boys of Ipswich Town to London Road. As usual and it's still the same today the glory fans came out for the big games as nearly 17,000 packed the ground but they were to be disappointed as the opponents returned with a 2-0 victory and another season in the basement league was on the cards with so many draws in games 8 in a row. But we did beat our new neighbours in the Football League Cambridge United winning 2-0 with Dennis Oakes and Richie Barker netting and for the first time you were apart from the away fans long gone where you could move round to the end you where kicking at half time. Great run of results at the end of the season including a home win by lone Peter Price at home against the Cobblers and trashing of Cambridge United at the Abbey with two goals each for Tommy Robson and Richie Barker and a Jim Hall strike. Jim Iley did not win the hearts of many posh fans while at the club but his run of late results saw him awarded with the April Manager of the Month for Division Four.

The club finished eighth in the division above Cambridge United and lowly Northampton Town. Another season in Division Four to look forward to league gates had averaged at just over 5,000 and top scorer Peter Price netted 28 times. The pre season of 1972/3 did not give the fans much hope for the coming season having to rely on the squad from last season plus two new signings of another Ray Smith this time a very run of the mill player not like the original and Bobby Park who did not get on the park very much excuse the pun both from Wrexham. The Checker Trade Trophy in those days was the Watney Cup we had some good early season cheer against Blackpool in the First Round in front of 7,600 in a Mickey Mouse competition then going out to then First Division side Sheffield United 4-0. In the first thirteen games of the campaign we only recorded one victory a 3-0 home victory against Doncaster Rovers in the dismal run was the clubs record defeat losing 8-2 away to Chester the game after this only 3,600 turned up watch us lose the local derby against the Cobblers.

During this run the club said good bye to Jim Iley and former full back of our Championship team of 1960/1 Jim Walker took over the reins on Caretaker basis form did not change and the club appointed Noel Cantwell former Manchester United, West Ham and Northern Ireland captain and centre half as the new manager he soon employed ex Nott's Forest and Arsenal half back John Barnwell as his assistant. He brought quality players in very quickly John Cozens from Nott's County, Aston Villa full back Keith Bradley firstly on loan and Eric Young on three months loan from Manchester United met Eric some seasons ago now a Policeman when we visited Hartlepool's United when he said he played for us did not think anybody would remember him he was a class player who's loan was too short.

The F.A. Cup brought us some relief from the league season Jim Hall netting in the last minute against the Cobblers then we travelled to Bishops Stortford after a 2-2 draw away Posh finished the job beating them 3-1 at home with Tommy Robson, Don Heath and Jim Hall netting in a game that saw later manager John Still playing for the losers. What a draw in the 3rd Round home against top dogs Derby County whose team was a collection of star studded names. Despite a spirited display in front of hostile County supporters in the gate of nearly 21.000 we only lost 1-0 to a Roger Davies strike. One of the most exciting games was the 6-3 home game with Barnsley we stormed into a early three goal lead but the Tykes pulled it back level and then before the break Posh scored two more to make it 5-3 at the break and finally 6-3 the scorers being Jim Hall hat trick, Chris Turner, Tommy Robson and John Cozens. The season finished with the club finishing in 19th position just above the re-election zone. The fans hailed Noel Cantwell as the Messiah and he was to bring great days back to the club again.

## HAIL THE MESSIAH

Noel Cantwell had a very busy close season bringing in Freddie Hill for £5,000 from Manchester City the best player in my opinion to play for the Posh now reaching the twilight of his career and holder of two England International caps. Jeff Lee and Dave Llewellyn completed his signings for the time being. David Gregory the local lad who playing for Walton against me always turned me inside out when playing full back against him was also added to the squad. What a season it was going to be Posh going all season to be undefeated at home and only letting in 10 goals at Fortress London Road. A good early start to the season saw us in the first six gates were going up and Noel Cantwell added Bert Murray after a loan for Chelsea he played for them when they beat us in the Sixth Round earlier.

A Jeff Lee penalty against Lincoln City took us into top spot and we held on to the spot to make it a Happy Christmas for the Posh and me and Anne as it was our dear daughter Sharon's first Christmas a time she always adored every year in her life and we will continue to do so. As well as success in the league we again had a great run in the FA cup beating Colchester United at then at the ageing Layer Road a far cry from their new stadium on the outskirts of the town now winning by 3-2 with goals from a John Cozens brace and Bert Murray. Second round we travelled to non league Wycombe Wanderers and their notorious sloping pitch at Old Loakes Park on a bitterly cold and windy day posh running out winners 3-1 with a brace from John Cozens and Jim Hall. Next up in the Cup this time at home were Southend United John Cozens and Freddie Hill put us 2-0 up at the break in front of nearly 12,000 fans and Tommy Robson completed the 3-1 victory.

Fans were now flocking back with the success of the team. Next home game the lure of tickets for the upcoming Fourth Round tie against the mighty Leeds United nearly 16,000 turned up to watch us held to a draw to Bradford City with Tommy Robson netting. Leeds United took no pity on us both with the selection of the team the whole team with the exception of Roy Ellam the reserve centre half all the team were internationals and they took no prisoners on the park just after the half hour mark they were 4-0 up through a Joe Jordan brace, Peter Lorimer and Terry Yorath but did allow us a consolation goal from John Cozens. Leeds fans will be remembered at this game for dismantling the tea hut at Moy's Lane End that was stacked on the running track no health and safety in those days but the game brought the club a big pay day 28,000 fans being present.

Perhaps the final piece of Noel Cantwells own team was the signing of goalkeeper Eric Steele on loan from Newcastle United replacing Mick Drewery Eric's career was to span to 148 games on the trot only being beaten by George Boyd many seasons later. Posh were now on the shirt tails of leaders Colchester United the lead now down to five points remember in those days two for a win after beating them at home 2-0 with goals from Jim Hall and John Cozens but because of the Cup run we had four games in hand over them. We were to have a set back at Gillingham losing 1-0 but little did we know the return game at London Road was to be forever remembered in the club's history at least by us older supporters.

With eight games left Noel Cantwell said that we needed another seven points from our eight games left to win promotion but better things were to come. The home game against Darlington saw a Freddie Hill goal think it was one of his trade mark free kicks saw us reach Noels first goal signalling the return of the Super Posh back to Division Three with three games in hand over some of our rivals and one point in front of Gillingham with a game in hand. Next game was the long journey North to Hartlepool's United can remember the coach being parked on what looked like a demolition site and wondered if we would have any windows for the journey home especially when a late goal from Tommy Robson on his own territory sealed at 1-0 victory and it made for a happy trip home still thankfully with windows intact.

The victory took us into second place with three games left to play Gillingham were top with only the Posh to play and we having three games left to seal the

Fourth Division title. May day don't think it was a public holiday in those days heralded the return to the Third Division with over 17,000 people witnessing it Gillingham taking the lead through an early penalty then flying Tommy Robson was brought down and Jeff Lee levelled from the spot and before the break John Cozens put us in front and after an hour giant Chris Turner headed us 3-1 in front and with under 20 minutes to go the Gills scored again to make it 3-2 but with the minutes ticking by John Cozens scored again to crown the POSH CHAMPIONS OF DIVISION FOUR and with two games still to play. The last two games being away the club arranged a game against an All Stars XI which included many big names in the game to aid the testimonial funds of former injured retired players Frank Noble and Bobby Moss so they could receive the trophy presented by Len Shipman who had an important role of getting the club demoted earlier and was not very popular with our fans. Needless to say that Noel Cantwell was awarded the Manager of the Season and Tommy Robson tells me they were drunk for two days after and Freddie Hill, Paul Walker and Jim Hall were nominated in the P.F.A Division Four Team but strangely not Tommy must have upset so many full backs falling over.

In my opinion the 1973/4 season and the team was one of the best I have seen. Could this team go on to even better things? The new season of 1974/5 started with Eric Steele signing on permanently for the club and Peter Price coming back on loan from Pompey a move that never worked out we had a good start to the season we hovered in the top six goals were at a premium and in the early games we had a rely on centre half Chris Turner scoring on several times mostly from corners. By the end of October we were top of the league with a 3-0 win against Bury at home with goals from John Nixon, Tommy Robson and again Chris Turner. Remember coming home from the Crystal Palace game to see John Galley on loan from Nottingham Forest score his lone goal for us in a 1-1 draw think it was our only shot in the game that was shown on Match of the Day.

The First Round of the F.A cup saw a marathon tie against Southern League Weymouth after a goalless draw at home we were very fortunate not to go out in the replay needing a Chris Turner goal in the last minute and then in the last minute of extra time our Welsh u23 international Dave Llewellyn netted adding to an early David Gregory goal to tie things up at 3-3. In those days it was not like today's cup games being decided by penalty shoot outs. The game went to a third replay at London Road but this time no slip up winning 3-0 with David Gregory scoring twice and Chris Turner. Because of the replays Posh played the next round only five days later against Charlton Athletic and saw we progress to

*A trip down memory lane, me starring as goal keeper for G.P.O. Sports beating Ryhall United 4-0 in the Peterborough Minor Cup Final in 1971/2 season. Our line up was back row Brian Hill, Player Manager Geoff Manning, Dick Wright, Yours truly, Mick Revell, Keith Snart; Front Row, Mel Sambells, Billy Adams, Graham Bussey, Skipper Phil Butler and Alan Turner.*

*Peter Bonetti The Cat alias me taking a kick in the mouth early doors from Mick Bull my favourite referee Bob Fielding running the line.*

the Second Round beating them 3-0 with Bert Murray, John Nixon and David Gregory netting. With us just remaining in the top half of the table and the goal that was to win our Third Round game at London Road against Tranmere Rovers was to come from an unlikely candidate full back Keith Bradley in front of nearly 10,000 fans which set up a fourth round game against non league Stafford Rangers held at Stoke City's old ground Victoria Park in front of over 31,000 went on the train and can remember being herded along by Police horses first time I had seen them used at a football match. The non league team went into an early lead and made us fight all the way but goals from John Nixon and the impressive Dave Gregory setting up a 2-1 victory.

The draw for the Fifth round game us a home game against high flying First Division Middlesbrough nearly 26,000 packed London Road and we looked if we were going to do another giant killing act as David Gregory was again our star man John Nixon scoring the early goal but they scored a leveller to take us back to the old Ayresome Park another long trek on a week night. The other Boro or the Smoggies dominated the replay and were worthy winners with two goals from their popular Allan Foggan lots of us Posh fans made the long journey north and the attendance was over 34,000. The Cup run had an effect on our league form not winning in four games and dropping below half way in the division. After a couple of good results we went to the Recreation Ground at lowly Aldershot and received a 5-0 trashing and remember all the glasses on the shelves in the bar vibrating as the trains went by near the stadium and with it fading hopes of promotion. The end of the season saw perhaps the worse bit of violence seen at a home game who were hoping to win the Third Division title with already being promoted Plymouth Argyle were the visitors. With me to catch the bus for work in town even at 7am the city was awash with the Pilgrims supporters some well oiled after staying over in the city over 5,000 of them made the 560 round journey could have longer then with not so many motorways hoping to beat us and this was not to be Tommy Robsons goal sealing their fate as runners up but not before their fans had invaded the pitch referee Mr Williams being hit with a bottle and then having a pitch battle on the pitch with the police. They were piped to the title by one point by Blackburn Rovers Posh finishing ten points behind in seventh place.

## BREAKING UP IS HARD TO DO.

Very fitting that Neil Sedaka released this song as a ballad in 1975 as the season 1975/6 was to see the see the Champions side of 1973/4 break up my favourite

# TERRY BLY

Signed from Norwich City in 1960 by Manager Jimmy Hagan, Terry was a very modest gentleman whose name is always mentioned today by those loyal supporters. Helped Posh to win the 4th Division Championship 1960/61 (first ever Season in the Football League). Terry scored a Club record 52 + 2 FA Cup goals (a 4th Division record). This includes 7 magnificent hat-tricks. A brave powerful player, a great header of the ball and equally as good with his feet.

## FACTFILE

| | |
|---|---|
| Born | 22nd October 1935, Fincham (King's Lynn) |
| Died | 24th September 2009 (aged 73) |
| Club Role | Player |
| Position | Centre-forward |
| Period with club | 1960-1962 |
| Appearances | 101 |
| Goals | 87 |
| Achievements | Division 4 Record Scorer 1960/61 |
| | Division 4 Champions 1960/61 |

INDUCTED 22ND NOVEMBER 2008

# 1960/61 DIVISION 4 CHAMPIONS

Arguably the best ever Posh side, winning the 4th Division Championship title in their first ever Football League Season, scoring a record 134 goals with Terry Bly leading goal scorer with a record of 52 League goals + 2 in the FA Cup. Also Terry's fellow four forwards; Billy Hails, Dennis Emery, Ray Smith and Peter McNamee each scoring well into double figures and not of course forgetting the wonderful defence led admirably by Captain Norman Rigby. They also enjoyed a wonderful Cup run away to 1st Division Aston Villa in the 4th Round replay, unlucky to lose 2-1 in front of an astonishing crowd of 64,531 people (this was the pulling power of Posh!). Managed by Ex-England and Sheffield United player Jimmy Hagan and trainer Ex-Manchester United player Johnny Anderson.

Pictured above left top right back row: Dick Whittaker, Keith Ripley, Jack Walls, Jim Walker, Terry Bly, Jim Rayner. Front row: Billy Hails, Dennis Emery, Norman Rigby, Ray Smith, Peter McNamee.

Also played: Roy Banham (15), Ellis Stafford (13), Derek Norris (5), Ray Hogg (2), Cliff Sansby (1), John Taylor (1), Jimmy Dunne (1), Jimmy Sheavills (1).

Induction presented to Ray Smith alongside his son on behalf of the 1960/61 squad.

INDUCTED 7TH MARCH 2011

# FREDDIE HILL

Signed from Manchester City in 1973 by Manager Noel Cantwell, Freddie helped Posh to win the 4th Division Championship in 1973/74. The ex-England international was a genius who oozed class and had superb vision. Freddie, who had trademark free kicks, was one of the best midfield players ever to appear for Posh. He was a joy to watch with his amazing skills. He was nicknamed 'Freddie The Fox' for his cunningness. A most popular member of the team both on and off the field with colleagues and fans alike.

## FACTFILE

| | |
|---|---|
| Born | 17th January 1940, Sheffield |
| Club Role | Player |
| Position | Midfield |
| Period with club | 1973-1975 |
| Appearances | 89 (86 + 3 sub) |
| Goals | 8 |
| Achievements | Division 4 Champions 1973/74 |

INDUCTED 20TH FEBRUARY 2010

# 1973/74 DIVISION 4 CHAMPIONS

A great experienced team led admirably by Ex-Manchester United and Eire Captain, Manager Noel Cantwell and Coach John Barnwell – Ex-Notts Forest and Arsenal. A confident team who played with passion and flare, especially when beating Gillingham at London Road, to secure the 4th Division Championship 4-2 on 1st May 1974 in front of a large crowd of 17,569. This was one of the most exciting League matches ever seen at London Road whilst maintaining their record of never losing a match at London Road that season.

Squad included: Eric Steele, Mick Drewery, Keith Bradley, Jeff Lee, Paul Walker, Chris Turner, Mick Jones, Bert Murray, Freddie Hill, Tommy Robson, John Cozens, Jim Hall, Jack Carmichael, Keith Oakes, David Gregory, David Llewellyn – also appeared Alan Lewis (on loan), Dougald McLachlan, Brendan Phillips.

Induction presented to Tommy Robson, Bert Murray and Dave Gregory on behalf of the 1973/74 squad.

INDUCTED 6TH SEPTEMBER 2014

# TOMMY ROBSON

Signed from Newcastle United in 1968 by Manager Norman Rigby, for a then record fee of £20,000, Tommy went on to help Posh win the 4th Division Championship in 1973/74 and becoming Player of the Season. He again took the accolade as Player of the Season in 1977/78. Tommy was awarded a Benefit Match in 1975/76 and a Testimonial in 1980/81 for his long service (of 13 years). Tommy has an abundance of skill, speed and scored spectacular goals. He later became Youth Team Coach in the mid-1980s. Worshipped by the fans who constantly sang out his name around the stadiums "We've got Tommy Tommy Tommy, Robson on the wing..." One of Peterborough United's favourite sons and an absolute crowd pleaser.

## FACTFILE

| | |
|---|---|
| **Born** | 31st July 1944, Gateshead |
| **Club Role** | Player/Youth Team Coach/Match Day Host |
| **Position** | Left-wing |
| **Period with club** | 1968-1981 (Player) |
| | 1983-1985 (Youth Team Coach) |
| | 2009 - Present (Match Day Host) |
| **Appearances** | 559 (514 + 45 sub) |
| **Goals** | 128 |
| **Achievements** | Record League Appearances 482 |
| | Division 4 Champions 1973/74 |

INDUCTED 4TH OCTOBER 2008

# CHRIS TURNER

The word 'legend' gets banded about quite regularly in sport, but Chris Turner can accurately be described as a Peterborough United legend. A whole-hearted defender, he started his playing career at Posh in 1969 and made more than 300 appearances, spending nine years with the football club before demonstrating he had the Midas touch by leading the city side to back to back promotions in the early 90s. Not only was he a hugely successful player and manager, Turner worked behind the scenes at the stadium in a host of roles before adding 'owner' to his unparalleled CV. But aside from all of the statistics and job titles, Turner was one of the nicest guys you could come across.

## FACTFILE

| | |
|---|---|
| **Born** | 3rd April 1951, St. Neots |
| **Died** | 27th April 2015 (aged 64) |
| **Club Role** | Player/Manager/Chairman/CEO/Sales Manager |
| **Position** | Defender |
| **Period with club** | 1969-1978 (Player)<br>1990-1992 & 1993/1994 (Manager)<br>1993-1996 (Chairman)<br>1994-1996 (Chief Executive Officer)<br>1996-1997 (Sales Manager) |
| **Appearances** | 364 (357 + 7 sub) |
| **Goals** | 43 |
| **Achievements** | Division 4 Promoted 1990/91<br>Division 3 Play-off Final Winner 1991/92 |

INDUCTED 5TH DECEMBER 2009

# KEN CHARLERY

Signed from Maidstone United in 1991 by Manager Chris Turner, Kenny scored twice to help Posh win the 3rd Division Play-Off Final against Stockport County at Wembley in 1992. He was Player of the Season and top goalscorer in 1991/92 and 1994/95. Nicknamed 'King Kenny' by fans for his goals. Kenny joined Watford in October 1992 (for then a Club record £350,000) and returned to Posh in December 1993. In July 1995 he joined Birmingham City, who were managed by Barry Fry, again for £350,000. He returned to Posh once more in February 1996 signing as a Player/Coach by Manager Mick Halsall.

Kenny with his daughter and teammates Noel Luke (far left) and Bobby Barnes (far right).

## FACTFILE

| | |
|---|---|
| **Born** | 28th November 1964, Stepney |
| **Club Role** | Player/Assistant Manager |
| **Position** | Centre-forward |
| **Period with club** | 1991-1992 (Player) |
| | 1993-1995 (Player) |
| | 1996-1997 (Player) |
| | 2005-2006 (Assistant Manager) |
| **Appearances** | 224 (216 + 8 sub) |
| **Goals** | 80 |
| **Achievements** | 3rd Division Play-Off Winner 1992 |

INDUCTED 18TH APRIL 2009

*Mark Tyler, who I'm sure will soon be in the Pos Hall of Fame.*
*Born Norwich 1977 – 40 year-old; Position Goalkeeper.*
*Joined Posh 1994 from Youth level.*
*Appearances 494,*
*Honours Div 3 Playoff 1999/00 Div 2 R/U 2007/8 Div 2 P.F.A. Team 2001/2.*

player Freddie Hill moved to Cork big Jim Hall moved to the Cobblers where he spent part of the previous season on loan ending a career at London Road playing 329 games and five as substitute and scoring 137 times 122 in the Football League a record that still stands today and was to be transferred for £4,500 what a bargain cheap as the Poundshop back to the team he joined us from he had another couple of seasons for them netting 28 times in 69 games

*George Boyd, who is not in the Hall of Fame as he's still playing.*
*Born Chatham 1985 – 31 year-old; Position, Striker.*
*Joined Posh 1st Jan 2007 – 28th May 2013.*
*Appearances 263, goals 64, Honours Runners Up Div 2 2007/8, Runners Up Div 1 2008/9.*
*Play off Div 1 2010/11 and PFA teams in 2007/8 and 2008/9.*

and then to Cambridge United 15 times in 24 games now living in Yarmouth and comes as Tommy Robeson's guest a couple times a season and in the Posh Hall of Fame. Paul Walker also moved on to be signed on by former manager Jim Iley at Barnsley.

Again a poor start to a season we did not win a game until we beat Wrexham in late September 2-0 at home with Tommy Robson and David Gregory netting. But we did make progress in the Football League cup easing past Southend United 3-0 despite losing the first leg at Roots Hall with goals from Chris Turner, Tommy Robson and John Cozens both legs with gates well over 4,000 a bit different to the early round attendances of today. Next up at London Road

## The Posh Affair

for Round Two were the tangerines of Blackpool and again we were the victors by 2-0 with second half goals from Dave Gregory and Tommy Robson. After a draw 2-2 with goals from Mick Jones and David Gregory away against Sheffield Wednesday, then struggling in Division Three after being relegated now under Jack Charlton.

Then we made the journey to Craven Cottage to take on Division Two Fulham in the Third Round of the League Cup Bobby Moore in their side and thanks to a David Gregory goal and some fantastic saves by Eric Steele we progressed to the Fourth Round. Draws were now the order of the day seven in ten games not helping our league position. A long trip to Middlesbrough left us with a long journey home well beaten 3-0. But a unbeaten run of eleven games saw us rise from mid table to second this was ended by a 5-2 thrashing at Cardiff City despite Lyndon Hughes and David Gregory netting the Bluebirds being promoted at the end of the season. Again the F.A. Cup was going to be the pinnacle of the season disposing of non league Winsford United with four second half goals with goals from Jon Nixon, John Cozens, Dave Gregory and Chris Turner at London Road the draw for the next round against Coventry Sporting held at Coventry City ground Highfield Road stadium saw no slip up recording a 4-0 victory Lyndon Hughes, Mick Jones, Jon Nixon and an own goal.

Round four saw us make the short journey to Nottingham Forest under Brian Clough to play out a goal less draw on a quagmire of a pitch Tommy Robson tells the story that sea gulls were in residence on the large puddles in the goalmouths. Nearly 18,000 turned up for the replay the only goal coming from mid way in the first half by Jon Nixon who had moved from neighbours Nott's County to the Posh. Posh made an addition to its forward line before the next round a trip to the great Manchester United to mark a return to manager Noel Cantwells old team when signed lanky centre forward Ernie Moss a prolific goal scorer from Chesterfield he had netted 67 times in 95 games for them even though he was not a great success at Posh he still managed nine goals in 35 games and went on to score 192 goals in 539 games less than a goal every three games in his career. Ernie now has Picks Disease a rare form of Dementia which could have been from constant heading of the ball as reported in his local media. The mass exodus of over 10,000 fans and followers from the city swelled the attendance at Old Trafford to over 53,000 but the game was over in the first ten minutes with goals from Alex Forsyth and Sammy McIlroy but a John Cozens goal before half time put us back in contention before Gordon Hill eased them in to a winning 3-1 margin and our reward was a massive pay day can remember all these youngsters sitting on walls trying to pinch our scarves as we came out of the ground.

After a run of good results after this game the wheels came off our promotion push and we slipped down the table our last 17 games only bringing two victories and we finished the season in 10th spot but a whole lot better off money wise. The new season heralded the signing on two players one who are among the greatest midfield players in Bobby Doyle signed from Barnsley and goalkeeper Keith Waugh a youngster signed from Sunderland they went on to make 130 and 192 league games respectively and Bobby Doyle was in P.F.A team of the season while at Barnsley in the previous season. Early season success again the 1976/7 season beating Reading after extra time over two legs this brought us a tie against the star studded Fulham at Craven Cottage a team with Bobby Moore, Rodney Moore and Alan Slough soon to be playing at the Posh. The game saw Posh earn a replay Bobby Doyle scoring in a 1-1 draw. The replay saw the best goal in my life scored at London Road by it had to be by George Best when he volleyed the ball in after a flick up in front of us on the Glebe Road to give Eric Steele as good a chance of winning the pools of stopping it.

Alan Slough added to it and even a late Tommy Robson did ease the pain of the greatest goal scored against us in front of over 16,000 present. After the Chesterfield game a 3-0 home loss in early October Noel Cantwell was running out of patience with his underperforming team now in 15th position and put all the players up for sale. A 6-2 defeat at Brighton saw the end of Eric Steele's posh career being replaced by the young Keith Waugh. The was a welcome break from the misfortunes of the league but after the sound beating of Tranmere Rovers 4-0 at Prenton Park with goals from John Cozens, Ernie Moss, Tommy Robson and yes Jack Carmichael his first for the club then he scored again in the next game at home to Sheffield Wednesday in a 2-1 defeat this was getting a bit of a habit no not really his 358 league games saw him find the net five times but a tremendous servant to the club. The next round of the FA cup was a big disaster for the team after the original game at non league Northwich Victoria being abandoned by fog with Posh winning by a Jon Nixon goal when the teams met again three days later we were humbled to the tune of a 4-0 defeat which has to be the clubs worst defeat against non league opponents. Things did not improve in the league and we struggled in the bottom half of the table after the home win against Northampton Town 3-1 with goals from John Cozens, David Gregory and full back Peter Hindley the last eight games of the season were winless and we finally finished 15th but perhaps the consolation that the Cobblers were relegated. The final nail in our season was the resignation of Noel

Cantwell after three years at the club his number two John Barnwell taking over the role never to be forgotten as one of the best managers the club have had but he was to return.

## LIFE AFTER THE MESSIAH

John Barnwell brought in new players most notable being the capture of Alan Slough from Fulham and experienced keeper Jim Barron ex Nottingham Forest and Wolves. Early season 1977/8 league form was not helped by us not finding the net again but again we had progressed well again in the Football League cup beating Bradford City over two legs and then needing two attempts to see off Scunthorpe United and going out finally Bolton's Burnden Park on a freezing night remember could see the Vaseline glistening on the players legs and we went down 3-1 despite an Alan Slough goal.

A 2-0 defeat of Cambridge United from Tony Cliss and Gary Sargent saw us go on 8 league games unbeaten run and rising to second place with Cambridge ending it 1-0 at The Abbey. In between we progressed in the F.A.Cup with First Round victory against Barnet at Underhill with Alan Slough and and Tommy Robson netting we needed two attempts to see off Gillingham with Alan Slough netting in the first game away and the goals in the return being scored by Jack Carmichael his only goal this after netting five times the previous one. After the loss to Cambridge United in the league Newcastle United were our opponents in Round Three and over 17,000 packed London Road as the visitors scored first only for Gary Sargent to level and set up a replay at St. James Park in front of nearly 26,000 on a terrible windy night can still remember keeper Jim Barron trying to clear the penalty area with his goal kicks and it snowed on the long haul home after a 2-0 defeat with goals from Ray Blackhall and Tommy Craig no consolation to us the Geordies were relegated to Division Two at the end of the campaign.

The lack of goals was costing us results and the middle of February saw us down in mid table but an eleven game unbeaten run including seven wins the highlight being the home trashing 5-0 of Bradford City with Tommy Robson two, Billy McEwan, Chris Turner and Trevor Anderson netting and it looked as though promotion was on the cards. But disaster was round the corner to go we needed to win all our four remaining games we started well with a lone Tommy Robson goal beating Tranmere Rovers then we were hit with a first half blitz by struggling Oxford United being three goals up after half an hour but goals from Tommy Robson, Chris Turner and Alan Slough netting from the spot levelled things up but we had lost a valuable point which was going to cost us dearly.

This scenario was going to continue at the penultimate game at Sealand Road then home of Chester City they scored early and then Alan Slough scored his first penalty after half an hour then Chester went into a 3-1 lead then two minutes later he scored his second spot kick then they scored again with six minutes to go and finally referee Bob Newsome awarded our third penalty and Alan Slough completed his hat trick and finished on the losing side one of the games that stands out in my memory as the next does the final game of the season at the Racecourse ground at Wrexham who were already champions and an army of Supporters Club made the long journey to Wales to swell the 23,000 crowd it was win or miss out on promotion the crowd swelled by Preston fans urging on the hosts because if we did not win them would go up Wrexham keeper Dai Davies had one of the games I have ever seen from a keeper can still see when Barry Butlin was clean through and saved by sticking out his leg and then a tremendous save from Tommy Robson the game finishing goalless and it was the only time have cried at a game we were all broken hearted and was not helped by the joyous fans of Wrexham and Preston celebrating. To make things worse Cambridge United finished second another bitter pill to swallow. At the end of the day 16 draws and only netting 47 goals cost us promotion.

**DIVISION FOUR ON THE HORIZON**

First shock of the 1978/9 season was the transfer of Chris Turner to Luton Town for £115,000 and in return signed from West Ham United Bill Green for £60,000 who never fitted the role of the great man he replaced to me one of the worse signings we ever made. Early season form was good and after First Round League Cup victory against Hull City over two legs we meet the now familiar opponents Middlesbrough firstly away in a goalless bore draw and then winning the replay at home in extra time with a header Tommy Robson a collector's item in his long Posh career. After a bad run of results manager John Barnwell's days looked numbered at the club and he resigned after the Board of Directors refused him funds to bring new players in after the defeat in the Fourth Round League Cup journey to Brighton the only goal being scored by Mark Lawrenson soon to join the hot seat at London Road. Former club winger Billy Hails took over the reins but he only lasted 12 games with the club in 20th place and claiming only one win he again wanted money for new players this was again refused.

Peter Morris who had a distinguished career playing for Mansfield, Norwich City and Ipswich joined as manager from Mansfield Town was going to be the third manager this season. Despite signing several players on perhaps on free transfer the season was slipping away and we never got out of the relegation zone and our fate was sealed with still two games to after a home scoreless draw at home to Chesterfield in front of over 2,000 fans and even less 1,875 witnessed the final rites a 3-0 win against Hull City last game defeat at Bury seems to ring a bell saw us relegated legally for the first time back to Division Four.

Peter Morris had a very busy 1979/80 close season with five players being shown the door all on frees but we got £30,000 welcomed money from the sale of Billy McEwan to Rotherham United bringing in Mick Lambert from Ipswich and Ian Phillips from Mansfield both his former clubs. Later selling fans favourite Bobby Doyle to Blackpool for £110,000 and using £25,000 to buy non league Kettering Towns Billy Kellock and Chesterfields Ricky Heppolette for £30,000 his Posh career being cut by an early seasons bad injury. Charlton were defeated over the two legged Football League Cup on 4-2 aggregate and a goalless home draw to Blackpool followed by a lone Billy Kellock goal from the spot in the replay then drawn at home to Bristol City in Round Three the game finished 1-1 Posh goal being scored by Andy Parkinson soon to do a runner from the club and in the replay we suffered a 4-0 defeat.

Now Peter Morris had young local lads in his side Mick Gynn and Trevor Quow and Steve Collins from Stamford all three went to forge a long career at Posh and beyond. We were putting a good run of results together and goals from Trevor Quow, Tommy Robson and the classy Billy Kellock who was to net 19 times during the season saw us reach third place against Crewe Alexandra. But then went a nine game winless win and by the end of the year we were below mid table 1980 started well with Dave Syrett who passed away in July 2016 with a brain tumour aged 60 scored twice and Jack Carmichael scoring his only strike of the season to beat Scunthorpe United 3-1.

Five wins on the bounce was started with a lone strike by Dave Syrett against Hereford United sitting in their new Edgar Road stand which was so steep it gave me vertigo and was glad when the game was over this winning run took us up to sixth place run coming to a end at run down Wigan's ground who did the double over us losing 2-1 with David Syrett netting. The next game brought one of the humours incidents that I can remember in my years of watching the Posh the goal that never was or was it in the game against Stockport County at home before the game Peter Morris was presented with the Manager of the Month in the Fourth Division for March which even now spells the kiss of death the next match this was not to be as young Tony Cliss supposedly netted at the London Road end the goal finishing up in the net through the side netting to the dismay of the County players the referee Mr Vickers and his linesman found the net intact despite the keeper asking a policeman for his verdict and it stood and the game finished 1-1.

Only two wins in the last five games saw dreams of promotion slip away and we finished in eight place with average attendance now down to just over 4,000 for the league season. The start of 1980/1 season saw as much change in the playing staff as boardroom with forward Robbie Cooke being signed from Grantham Town later to be joined by former Fen Man Jackie Gallagher from Wisbech also the club Chairman Mr Geoff Woodcock of the Woodcock Hotel along Bridge Street stepped down with Mr Hugh Wright replacing him. Robbie Cooke soon opened his account scoring twice over the Football League Cup 1st Round legs against Fulham Posh going through on 4-3 aggregate over the two legs after extra time. He also netted in the first two league games but the first victory at Doncaster Rovers to the tune of 4-0 with goals from local lad centre half Trevor Slack, Dave Syrett, Billy Kellock and David McVey also in the team was the stylish mid field player signed from Oxford United Gordon Hodgson.

In the Second Round of the League Cup we played Nottingham Forest over two legs now they were European Champions and over ran us 3-0 in the first leg in front of 16,000 with goals from John Robertson, Gary Birtles and Frank Grey doing the damage and despite a spirited display in the return leg which ended 1-1 with Gary Mills scoring for the Reds and Robbie Cooke for the Posh and it was back to the bread and butter of the league. A five win run in October pushed us up to third place then we had a run of six games without a win pushing us down to 7th but that was all going to change at The Shay the grimy home of Halifax Town complete with speedway track and pits in front of just over 1,100 fans we returned to winning ways with Robbie Cooke, Mick Gynn, and Billy Kellock netting and the Shay men finished bottom but one. In the F.A Cup 1st Round we were victors over the Cobblers Tommy Robson scoring a pair and Trevor Quow and Trevor Slack netting in a 4-1 win at the old County Ground and a couple of weeks later ran up a 3-0 home victory in the league against them with Billy Kellock, Robbie Cooke and Tommy Robson netting in between these two games we had disposed of Barnet in Round Two of the cup through a lone Tommy Robson strike.

Another great Cup run was on the cards we needed two attempts to beat Chesterfield in Round Three Robbie Cooke scoring in a 1-1 draw at London Road and scoring both goals in a 2-1 win on an unwelcoming January night at Saltergate. League form was holding up despite the interest in the Cup and we went into Round Five with a plumb home game v Manchester City nearly

28,000 packed London Road the crowds at both ends now watching through grills put up to put off threat of hooligans. After missing some early chances Tommy Booth scored the only goal of the game the papers said it was a shot but I seem to remember it was rebounds off his bum never mind they all count the only consolation was a bumper pay day for the Posh.

The memory of the game was soon forgotten a bit like the recent trip to Chelsea and our away days at Wembley having a five game run without a win ending with a 4-1 win against Tranmere Rovers with Billy Kellock netting twice, and local lads Mick Gynn and Trevor Slack in front of 3,000 odd fans and on the verge of a promotion position with the first four teams being promoted. We hung on by our shirt tails and our hopes were dented by the Cobblers at County Ground with two games to play Posh fighting back from two goals down with goals from Robbie Cooke and Colin Foster to force a draw still remember the half Spion Kop they had behind the goal and the cricket side of the ground.

The last home game a draw against Hartlepool's United meant that were to remain in Division Four finishing in fifth spot two points below Wimbledon who claimed the last promotion spot a position to be repeated next season. Season 1981/2 saw Tommy Robson being released but he was going to return in other roles at the club at a later date and if still kicking around on match days now he left with the record number of appearances 442 starts and netting 111 league goals only bettered by Jim Hall his great friend. Sponsorship was now creeping into sport and our first sponsor was local fizzy drink firm Sodastream. Peter Morris signed on Colin Clarke from Ipswich Town and he was capped many times in his posh days for Northern Ireland and Billy Rodaway and Steve Massey on free transfers and after the pre season tournament Keith Waugh departed for Sheffield United for £90,000 what a bargain even in those days.

He was replaced by a loanee from Nottingham Forest Lee Smelt he went as quickly as he came and he was replaced by Neil Freeman who was signed from Birmingham City. Early season form was average we went out of the Football League cup at the first hurdle losing over two legs to Barnsley gates again were poor only 3,700 odd watching us run riot against Rochdale winning 5-1 in early September with a hat trick from Robbie Cooke and goals from Trevor Slack and Trevor Quow after two long trips up north in successive weeks a goalless draw at Darlington sitting on the old bench seats in the main stand trying to avoid splinters in our bums but what a lovely old ground no longer with us in the league and a new ground sitting idle football wise. The other game at Hartlepool's saw a Billy Kellock goal claiming a win and that took us on a march up to with a run of four wins the best being the trashing of Aldershot at London

Road with Dave Syrett and Steve Massey netting twice in the 7-1 victory the local Derby against the Cobblers was settled by a lone Billy Kellock strike.

The FA Cup came to an end in Round Three after wins in the earlier rounds against Halifax away and Walsall at home but Bristol City put us out at London Road by a lone goal if we had won we would have had a money spinning game against Aston Villa the cost of which we were going to see the next season. The next league game was to see a heavy defeat at Wigan by 5-0 but then a run of 11 games unbeaten the best game if not performance but memory was the 4-4 draw home to Hartlepool's United and it was valuable points dropped now two as now three points for a win despite a hat trick from Robbie Cooke who finished the season with 29 goals in all games and Mick Gynn. We were now in the race for promotion again up to third place. York City ended the run beating us 4-3 away. The 1,000 league game saw us beat Torquay United 1-0 the goal coming from centre half Tony Smith the next home game was recorded on Anglia T.V. a 1-0 victory over Bury the winner coming from full back Ian Phillips bet we did get much television money in those days think it would have been Gerry Harrison doing the commentary.

The season was now going to go horribly wrong again at the final hurdles after creeping up to second place the visit of Sheffield United heralded the start of thinks going down 4-0 ever rivals the Cobblers did not help us out next game Posh losing by a lone goal. The next game was a battle royal at Colchester United's Layer Road a massive punch up saw centre half Tony Smith and a Colchester player sent and a lot of homework for referee Mr. Taylor booking six others despite the Posh lads trying to hide our culprit he did finally find him and flashed the red card Dave Syrett coming up with our equaliser. Our final hopes were all but dashed by another defeat at home to Wigan Athletic 3-0 most fans had brought match and coach tickets for the last game of the season at Sheffield United hoping to see us be promoted but that turned out to be a damp squib as defeat at Hereford United 2-1 and then going to a dead rudder at the Blades going down 4-0 and we finished the season bridesmaids again instead of the bride and thousands of our fans seeing them win the Division Four trophy. For the last dead game to both sides only just under 1,900 bothered turning up to see us lose to Tranmere Rovers 2-1 a Trevor Slack goal bringing the curtain down with us finishing fifth once again.

Early close season of 1982/3 did not change the fortunes and the mood at the club no money again and the Reserves and Youth teams were disbanded and Peter Morris was not amused after being such a successful manager perhaps in the top four I would name at the club. Posh then went to save money again with

# The Posh Affair

a Martin Wilkinson being appointed manager he was previously Alan Clarkes number two at Leeds United he went back to his old club to sign a young keeper David Seaman and centre half Neil Firm. From day one the season was going to be one of turmoil not helped with Billy Kellock leaving going to Luton Town for much welcomed funds with the first game of league at London Road against Hartlepool's united attracting just fewer than 3,500 with worse to come Posh winning with goals from full back John Winters and Ivor Linton. I myself was helping swell the crowd and now taking Sharon and her friend to home games sitting them on the Glebe Road wall they both liked afro haired Trevor Quow who returning after a broken leg he looks a bit different now. Neil Firm and Trevor Slack did not cover themselves in glory Firm on his Posh debut both being sent off at Stockport County despite this the nine men managed to draw 1-1 through Trevor Benjamin.

Wilkinson was now joined by Bill Harvey as right hand man and physio which he had done for a season before and was very well known in the football fraternity. We progressed through the First Round of the League Cup beating Darlington over two legs and then go out to Crystal Palace in Round Two. Goals and wins were at a premium in the first fifteen games we only managed three wins three home wins against Hartlepool's United, Bristol City and Halifax Town again we had a decent FA Cup run beating Chesterfield at the second attempt at home 2-1 with goals from Robbie Cooke and Mick Gynn, then in the next round Doncaster Rovers were on the end of a 5-2 beating Robbie Cooke with a brace and Colin Clarke, Trevor Quow and Mick Gynn netting. This result was a spring board for a change of results four wins on the trot and when we travelled to Luton Town we were up to mid table but our FA Cup interest was to end at Kenilworth Road on the wrong end of a 3-0 result.

News was that Noel Cantwell could be persuaded to return with things as bad on the field as in the boardroom especially as only 1,600 fans turned up to see us lose 1-0 and sink to 14th place. To balance the books Robbie Cooke was transferred to Cambridge United for £20,000 he is often to be seen at our matches scouting. Local lad Mario Ippolito who lived at the end of my street in Old Fletton and actually signed for me at Stanground United when I was player/ manager at the end of his career but never played a game was brought into the team at scored on his debut against Tranmere Rovers in a 3-0 with also Colin Clarke and Mick Gynn netting then he scored two in next game away to Halifax but he soon disappeared from the scene Martin Wilkinson tended his resignation with Posh in 13th position and speculation was that Noel Cantwell would and wanted to come back.

My Sharon's Uncle Bill Harvey took over and his caretaker role was going take him to the end of the season. With W.B.A. being reluctant to release John Wile to take over. Best game in Bills short reign and exciting one was the thriller at home to Swindon Town winning 4-3 after being 4-1 up at half time with goals from Trevor Slack, Phil Chard, Colin Clarke and Mick Gynn but they had to wait another four games for next win beating Blackpool 3-0 then two more wins against Mansfield and Hereford United and a last day defeat at Darlington 4-3 saw us finish in 9th place. It was confirmed that John Wile was going to take over from next season return of a great player but what could he produce as a manager we would soon know. Worrying fact that gates were down to 2,796 averages for league games just under 2,000 down on last season's average.

**WILE'S WOES**

The first signing John Wile brought in from his old club was Martin Pike and local lad Steve Collins departed for Southend United also fans were not pleased as Mick Gynn was to join Coventry City for £60,000, but rough house forward Ray Hankin joined from Middlesbrough that was previously was a great striker with Burnley. The first game saw us beat Hartlepool's United at home 3-1 with goals from Colin Clarke, David Buchanan and Ian Benjamin on the Tuesday night we travelled to Crystal Palace in the First Round of the League Cup sorry the Milk Cup and returned with a 3-0 hiding but managed to turn things around at London Road with a penalty shoot out after extra time Ray Hankin, Colin Clarke and Trevor Quow scoring in normal time. But did not get much further going out to Stoke City going down 2-1 on aggregate but plenty of drama bad boy Ray Hankin not only did he get the quickest yellow card ever seen at London Road but before the hour he was sent off when Mickey Thomas took a dive but he also had an early bath later in the match.

A six match unbeaten run sandwiched in between a loss to Oxford United in the First Round of the F.A. Cup which was very unusual also in the run young goalkeeper Steve Zenchuk who only went to help with the kit was thrown in the deep end when David Seaman got injured in the warm up and he helped Posh to a 2-1 victory at Bloomfield Road his only game for the club worked with him at Ideal World This took us up to second place with a home win against Colchester United in front of the biggest gate of the season on Boxing Day even gates on Bank Holidays today don't ever seem to improve Posh recording a 2-0 victory with goals from lanky Alan Waddle and Kenny Beech. The run came to an end against the Cobblers away a goal from Alan Waddle not being enough in a 2-1 defeat to make it worse Ray Hankin was sent off again. Lack of goals saw us go six games without a win and slip to mid table turning things around at home to Bury with a couple of Ian Benjamin goals. But Wile was not happy with his strike force and we loaned Garry Worrall from Manchester United on a month's loan and he came on as substitute against Mansfield Town as he kept place in the to start the next game against Reading with Alan Waddle scoring in a 1-1 draw at Elm Park. Next home game was a real confidence builder against Bristol City who was well in the mix for promotion winning 4-1.

The game against Aldershot saw Ray Hankin take his fourth early bath of the season and his days seemed numbered at the club being fined a couple of weeks wages and we went down 2-1 our goal being scored by John Wile this almost ended the clubs interest in promotion. Wile signed untried forward Errington Kelly from Coventry City and he scored on his debut along with Ian Benjamin, Gary Worrell and Phil Chard. Fourth division was assured with a 2-0 defeat at York City they were to go on to win the division now falling through the National League trapdoor even the 6-0 defeat of the Cobblers with a brace from Alan Waddle who was to finish our top scorer with 12 league goals and a couple from Errington Kelly, Jimmy Holmes and a rare Paddy Rayment strike. The fans were now talking with their feet and only 3,480 watched the local derby. The season was wrapped up with the two last home games with a 2-2 draw against Darlington with Trevor Slack and Trevor Quow netting and the final game versus Chester City Errington Kelly netting with both attendances being less than 2,000 the seasons average being just under 3,500. Would things have been different if Errington Kelly had joined sooner his 7 goals coming in 11 games or if Ray Hankins was able to stay on the park and not be constantly suspended?

1984/5 Six players were shown the door by John Wile but he managed get Trevor Slack, Trevor Quow and Phil Chard to sign new contracts. The season opened with a win against Tranmere Rovers with Jimmy Holmes netting our interest in the Milk Cup or Football League Cup ended at the first hurdle losing over two legs to Sheffield United losing by the odd goal at Bramhall Lane and despite winning 2-1 at home with goals from Francis Cassidy signed from Watford in close season and Errington Kelly an extra time goal saw the Blades go through. On my own front had now hung my boots up after spending a couple of seasons managing Stanground United in the old Peterborough Sunday league and now spending most evenings after work and long runs on Sundays could not miss my Posh dates pounding the streets and started me on a long running career people could say in football you were a decent player but it was the players around you as well but with running and the times you did told people you were a decent runner it was your own efforts.

So now Anne did not only have to put up with the Posh it was my running as well but she could understand that and her and Sharon Anne in my days in the colours of Werrington Joggers where I was club captain and was elected into their Hall Of Fame in 2009 went all over the country with supporting me. The second home game saw us beat Mansfield with a lone Errington Kelly goal and sent us on ten game unbeaten run and took us up to fourth place. Very early exit in the First Round away to non league Dagenham game remembered by many as the wall behind the goal where Posh fans were standing collapsed play was help up while it was cleared but reaction was that the referee did not add enough time on Posh went out by the only goal but it could have been a lot worse but thankfully no fans were injured. Greg Sheppard opened his account after being signed from Southend United in the local derby against Northampton Town in front of a poor Boxing Day crowd at the County Ground with Errington Kelly and Gary Worrell also netting in a 3-0 win. Three wins on the bounce with victories over Cambridge United, Wrexham and Torquay United then we went on a ten match run without a win during this run Ray Hankin was given his cards after being sent off at Port Vale and by the end of it we were down in the division to 10$^{th}$ place. The season was now slipping away once again at even the home local derby against the Cobblers which neither side found the net and was watched less than 2,500 fans surely the all time low for this derby. We could only find one victory in the last in the last eight games against Chester City 3-1 and only 1467 witnessed the home game against Aldershot on the Glebe Road you needed a pigeon to talk to the nearest person. The season saw us finish in 11th place with average gates just over 3,500.

1985/6 Close season saw the releasing of ten players through the revolving doors at the club Jackie Gallagher was resigned and his career was to be a great success this time around and later Lil Fucillo joined from Southend United and Andy Kowalski from Doncaster Rovers after having a long career at Chesterfield previously. First game of season at home to former giants Preston North End now in the bottom tier Posh recorded a 4-2 victory with two goals each from Jackie Gallagher and Gary Worrall and by the middle of end of September we were in second spot with beating Torquay United at home 2-0 with Andy Kowalski and Trevor Quow scoring. John Wile made the announcement that we has retiring from playing but did play a few games later in the season later signing centre half Wakely Gage from Chester City to replace him. Previous to this Posh were to receive a trashing from the Cobblers 5-0 at London Road not helped by keeper John Turner being sent off being replaced by on field player Jimmy Holmes no substitute keepers on the bench then he produced the worst stand in performance I have ever seen played like a man with two left arms he was useless. A couple of weeks later we were going to lose to our other local rivals Cambridge United 3-1 at The Abbey with Jimmy Holmes scoring as we seemed in free fall the next game losing 7-0 away to Tranmere Rovers without keeper John Turner who was suspended this still stands as the club biggest defeat in the Football League.

The only thing keeping the season alive was a good F.A. Cup run which started with a banana skin tie against non league Bishops Stortford the first game away finishing 2-2 with Posh winning the replay 3-1 with an early goal from Francis Cassidy and very late goals from Jackie Gallagher and Andy Kowalski to see off a very spirited display by The Blues. Second round we were drawn at home to another non league side Bath City and a lone Jackie Gallagher saw us safely through. League form was still bad and at the time we were drawn at home to home draw against Leeds United now not such a force now in Division Two with the attendance set at just 10,000 because of Leeds United bad image. In today's climate the game would have not been played with the pitch being so icy and later snow the hero was going to be early substitute Greg Sheppard scoring with a header Posh were later to have John Turner carried off with a broken leg that finished his career.

The new Freight Rover Trophy went as quick as it came as we crashed 4-1 at the Abbey Stadium to the Us and in the 4th Round of the Cup Carlisle made the 220 odd mile hike to the city and it must felt a lifetime going home with Greg Sheppard scoring the only goal yet again. The Fifth Round drew us at home to Brighton and Hove Albion over 15,000 packed into snow bound London Road to see Errington Kelly and Greg Shepherd net in a 2-2 draw other big teams were having a hard time the game before the replay against once proud Burnley now in Division four was witnessed by less than 3,000 fans Posh securing a draw with Trevor Slack scoring and Posh in 19th place. The replay at Goldstone Ground saw the Seagulls go through with a Dean Saunders goal. The memory of the past game had gone by the next League game only 1,500 turning up for the visit of Tranmere Rovers Posh losing by a lone goal. Even the local derbies against the Cobblers away could only bring in a mere 3,300 odd in a 2-2 draw with Errington Kelly and Trevor Slack scoring and against Cambridge United at home a goalless draw less than 3,000 attended. The game against Stockport County was a battle royal with three players getting red cards Andy Kowalski if I remember scored from his own half when the County keeper was dazzled by the sun and the ball bounced over his head and Greg Sheppard scoring very early. Worse attendance at London Road was the 279 who turned up to watch the dead rubber game against Aldershot Posh winning the meaningless game 2-0 a bit like the Barnet game this season in the dreaded Checkertrade Trophy.

Re election still seemed on the cards and a 5-0 thumping at Colchester United did not help our cause with three games to go in 19th position but two wins in the last two games against Aldershot witnessed by under 2,000 winning 3-0 with an Own goal, Lil Fuccillo and Jackie Gallagher netting and a 1-0 win at Mansfield Town with Trevor Quow scoring at then scoring again against Rochdale to draw 1-1 and bringing the curtain down on another poor season with average gates at London Road 2,584 just under 60,000 passing through the turnstiles for the league season. Things had to change. The start of 1986/7 season was to start with John Wile in the hot seat but it was going to be a short season for him local lads Trevor Slack went to Rotherham and Trevor Quow went off to Gillingham and my match day colleague Noel Luke alias Doris joined from W.B.A along with big Les Lawrence and Brynn Gunn from Nottingham Forest in all nearly signed a new team on. Money mostly coming from the new Lifeline imitative Wile also brought Tommy Robson back as Youth Team Manager.

After a win in the opening game home to Southend 2-0 with Les Lawrence opening his account for the club and Greg Shepherd netting the Football League Cup now the Littlewoods Cup saw us reach Round Two after beating Colchester United over two legs 2-0 with goals in the second leg from Noel Luke and an own goal. Second round we exited against Norwich City on 1-0 aggregate over the two legs season. In the early season derby against the Cobblers away losing 2-1 with David Gregory netting a season that they would finish as champions of the Fourth Division a loss to Crewe Alexandra next game put us in the bottom four and the writing was on the wall for manager John Wile.

Things were as bad off the field as on it with three directors resigning and a fourth did later in the season the reason being the debt of £400,000 and in the bottom four in today's game that figure would not get you a decent player. Fans were now demanding that John Wile should go they had their wish as he was sacked soon after the club A.G.M. By what was left of the Board of Directors. The club was in a bad place down in 19th position, sad that a man who had been such a great player for the club could not cut it as a manager. His player/coach Lil Fucillo was put in the hot seat as Caretaker Manager, rumour was rife that Noel Cantwell was coming back as manager after having spells managing in the states with New England Tea Men. Fucillo got off to a winning start at home to Tranmere Rovers 2-1 with the gate a mere 1,800. We fell at the first hurdle in the F.A. Cup to the Cobblers at the County ground 3-0 which yielded a good attendance of over 9,000 with them going great guns in the league.

There were some big teams in the division and we defeated Preston North End in Noel Cantwell first home 2-1 after the speculation became fact with goals from Noel Luke who rates him the best manager he played under at the club and new signing Steve Phillips joining from Southend United. Mick Jones joined as Cantwells number two not Chris Turner as was speculated locally. Fans were now showing faith in the Messiahs return and over 4,000 saw the 1-1 draw with Scunthorpe United on Boxing Day Noel Luke netting for the Posh. No doubt that best result of the season was against another giant beating Wolverhampton Wanderers yes in Division Four at Molineaux in front of a very meagre crowd winning 3-0 with goals from Steve Phillips, Jack Gallagher and Noel Luke and the next game at home to Cambridge United with a 2-1 with goals Noel Luke and a resigned Errington Kelly.

The hype dropped off a bit when we did not win in four games including the defeat at home by the Cobblers which I will always remember as the day my Sharon's adopted Granddad Bill Harvey saved young cheeky full back Steve Collins life after he had a bad fall in the game and was knocked unconscious and swallowed his tongue but Bill had a instrument in his bag of tricks for this happening but that was soon behind us and we went on a crazy run of ten games without a defeat including seven victories during this run Cantwell was awarded the Manager of the Month and had embarked on raising £100,000 to buy new players in his Cantwell Crusade. After the run Posh were up to Fourth place the run coming to an end at Rochdale with a great turn out of posh fans making the 300 mile round journey to Spotland losing 3-2 David Gregory scoring a brace.

The wheels started to come off the promotion challenge now a playoff position the home game with Wolverhampton Wanderers being a must win game for both teams. A crowd of 9,500 packed the ground and the only goal was scored very early by Steve Bull the burly Wolves centre forward after reaching the play off final they were beaten by Aldershot. The Posh fairy story of the Messiah returning and leading us instant promotion was not to be the club finally finishing tenth.

**ARE THE GOOD TIMES RETURNING**

Cantwells Crusade funded the signing of legend Mick Halsall joining the club from Grimsby Town and later Mick Gooding joined from Rotherham at the start of the 1987/8 campaign along with David Riley on loan from Nottingham

Forest. Not the start of the season we were hoping for only wins against Carlisle United at home on the first day of the season with Mick Gooding opening his account and Steve Phillips netting the sole goal in the victory over Cambridge United we lost three games on the bounce but a Mick Gooding penalty earned us a home draw against mighty Wolverhampton Wanderers only just over 3,000 attended in the Littlewoods cup we had seen off Chesterfield in Round One 3-2 on aggregate and then Plymouth Argyle in Round Two 5-2 aggregate.

The crisis on the field did not end there the club still being £400,000 in the red. News of a businessmen looking to save the club came to nothing and a administrator was appointed was this to be the end of our beloved Posh and were we going to lose our Messiah and on top of this Chairman Steve Kendrick resigned. In round three of the Littlewoods Cup we faced Reading at home which resulted in a goalless draw and we went down 1-0 at Elm Park in the replay. Secretary Arnold Blades who gave many years service to the club in very troubled times instigated a SOS Posh to save our beloved club hoping on raise £500,000 the first two days saw £100,000 promised to keep us in business. The clubs future was assured by the City Council but not before three directors stood down including our own Alf Hand things must have been bad. The trouble was not helping things on the park but we did have success in the F.A. Cup beating Cardiff City at home 2-1 with a brace from Mick Gooding in between the cup rounds we a great victory over Burnley at home 5-0 with Mick Gooding scoring two again along with goals from Alan Parris, Steve Collins and Errington Kelly but despite this we were in the bottom half of the table. But worse things were to come in the Second Round of the F.A. we were humbled at home by non league Sutton United the first time ever on our own soil losing 3-1

December form as it still has been most seasons was abysmal losing at home the only point we collected was from our first visit to the Seamer stadium at Scarborough Noel Luke netting in a 1-1 draw and end of 1987 we were in 17th place. The first two games on successive days produced two wins to start the New Year a 3-1 away win to Cambridge United Mick Halsall, Noel Luke and a helping hand from a Us players scoring and then a 2-0 home victory over Cambridge United with Dale White and Noel Luke netting. Rumours were rife that the club was going to be taken over by a consortium but never came to anything but the club were fined for irregular payments to players this time £2,500 and not demotion like before thought to be about the signing of Mick Gooding. Finally we thought our club was saved when the City Council were to coughed up a £1,500,000 deal to save our beloved team but this latter failed due to a new Environment bill. The top performance of the season the away win at Wolverhampton Wanderers who finished as Champions with a late Mick Gooding goal at one of my favourite stadiums securing the points but despite putting a run of six wins in the last eight games we finished in seventh in the division. Mick Gooding must have been very pleased with his season's tally of 24 goals in the season and he was nominated in the seasons P.F.A. Fourth Division Team.

**THE DEVANEY YEARS**

New season new Chairman and guess what he was Irish John Devaney seems very familiar, he pumped £800.000 to clear the club debts and promised another £400,000 for team building also we had a new manager Noel Cantwell moving over to become General Manager and his assistant Mick Jones took over as team manager for the 1988/9 season. Among the new signings were local lads Dominic Genovese and Craig Goldie Goldsmith who previously was playing for me at Stanground United on Sunday afternoons with his brother Ernie both class players. Later to sign Dave Langan and Gerry McElhinney first game of the season is one you want in good weather the 450 round trip to Carlisle United with Mick Gooding scoring both goals in a 2-2 draw.

We managed to squeeze by W.B A. in the Littlewoods Cup aggregate score 3-2 but we did not get our first victory till match seven in the League with Craig Goldsmith netting the lone home goal against Stockport County in that run also going out of the Littlewoods Cup in Round Two to Leeds United losing 2-1 at home and 3-1 at Elland Road. We could not put two wins together the home wins against Burnley 3-0 with Craig Goldsmith, Nick Cusack and Keith Oakes scoring and the game home to Hereford United broke the mould with a 2-1 win with Nick Cusack and David Longhurst doing the damage. Followed by a 5-0 hammering at Halifax Town was the F.A. Cup going to change our fortunes it took an extra time own goal in the First Round replay after a 3-3 draw at home to see us through and we needed a replay at Brentford but despite goals from Mick Halsall and Nick Cusack our interest ended in Round Two the Bees winning 3-2. Neighbours Cambridge United wished Posh a Happy New Year trashing us 5-1 at home with giant Dion Dublin going home with the matchball. We went on another winless run of seven games but that ended turning the tables over Halifax Town 2-1 at home with Nick Cusack and Keith Oakes netting now two places off the bottom.

The club made the signing of Worrell Sterling from Watford for £70,000 then a club record and what a player he would turn out to be. Posh needed to put some results together very quickly as Sharon Anne was going to see them relegated in her first season of travelling away. Three wins on the trot saw our situation improve a 3-0 win at home to Torquay United with David Longhurst netting twice and Worrell Stirling followed by a 1-0 home win over Wrexham with Nick Cusack scoring and an away win at Stockport County 2-1 with Noel Luke and Bryn Gunn on target. A home win against Crewe Alexandra about assured safety winning 3-2 Bryn Gunn scoring from the spot which he did six times in the league campaign now we can't even buy a spot kick Worrall Stirling and Noel Luke completed the scoring. The season finished with the club in 17th position a truly disappointing season which promised so much but only gave us a fight against relegation.

Mr Devaney again pledged money to Mick Jones in 1989/90 season top signing centre half Dave Robertson from Halifax Town for club record of £100,000. The season started against Maidstone United a team that fielded Ken Charley and Gary Cooper in it a lone Mick Halsall goal saw us take the points. The writing was on the wall for John Wile with us crashing out of the Littlewoods cup 6-4 on aggregate after extra time at Aldershot. Assistant David Booth replaced him very briefly then the Chairman announced he was going to bring a big name it was to be Mark Lawrenceson, we stayed in a mid table position with a lot of draws but the trilling 4-3 home victory over Exeter City who finished as champions with David Harle, Worrell Stirling, Milton Graham whose career was soon going to end so early with a serious knee injury his goal being one of the best scored at London Road behind the great George Best and a helping hand from a City defender was going to set up a run of nine league games undefeated in the league and victory over non league Hayes after a replay a Dave Robinson goal putting us through but going out in Round Two to Swansea City.

Now up to seventh but Cambridge United put an end to things at the Abbey winning 3-2 goals from Steve Osborne and Mick Halsall not enough. December was our usual damp squib not winning a single game and the fans had to wait to the end of January for the next win against Doncaster Rovers 2-1 with Keith Oakes and Worrell Stirling netting. We now had a new strike force David Riley joining from Nottingham Forest and the bulky Ronnie Jepson on loan from Port Vale and scored his first league goal in the 3-0 defeat of Carlisle United and both he and David Riley were on target along with Phil Culpin in the home 3-1 win against Wrexham. Jepson scored in the local derby a 1-0 wins over Lincoln City the locals were not very happy and we had to make a quick exit their season was finely balanced like ours. The 4-1 victory at home to Burnley lifted us to

8th with Mick Hassall, David Riley, Dave Robinson and Ronnie Jepson netting. A run of five games without as loss was to give us fans false hope Cambridge United once again did not help our cause beating us 2-1 with Worrell Sterling netting if front of over 9,000 fans a bitter pill to swallow and the season fizzled out with us finishing in 9th position despite the backing of Mr Deveneys cash we again had not achieved.

**CHRIS TURNS IT AROUND**

Mark Lawrenson was still in hot seat at the start of the 1990/1 season his only signings were George Berry ex Wolves and Kevin Bremner early form was patchy but we did knock Fulham out of the Rumbelows Cup 4-1 on aggregate. Kevin Russell joined from Leicester City on loan and he scored the only goal on his debut against Walsall on a sad day for football with the sudden death on the field of former player David Longhurst playing for York City with a serious heart condition often think how medical conditions have moved on would he have been saved in the present era. We have a plaque in the family stand at London Road to him and York City has a stand named after him taken so young at 25 years old. Russell was to net also in the next two wins a 2-0 victory along with Paul Culpin against Halifax Town and in the Cobblers derby beating them 2-1 Culpin again netting.

We did not survive in the Littlewoods Cup very long going out to Q.P.R. 4-2 on aggregate. By the start of November the club were in a good position in seventh place beating Chesterfield 2-1 with goals from George Berry and Mark Hine this time at home we all not knowing what the last game of the season would bring. The Leyland DAF Trophy at home to Cambridge United losing 2-0 was too much for Mark Lawrenson to stomach and he tended his resignation. His assistant David Booth was now in charge as Caretaker Manager. One of first games or games was facing Hereford United three times in less than drawing 1-1 in the First Round of the F.A. Cup at Edgar Street with David Riley scoring the replay three days later got us trough with goals from Riley again and Worrell Stirling then at weekend we shared a no score draw again at Edgar Street. This result put us in sixth place. Who can forget the snow covered pitch at Adams Park in the Second Round when the game against Wycombe Wanderers was called off and John Motson standing on the pitch telling us the news can't remember if the coaches arrived. We could not get a win when the game was staged mid week with Phil Culpin scoring an equaliser and it was back to London Road and a 2-0 win with Culpin and Mick Halsall netting.

A six game blip including defeat 2-1 defeat against Port Vale in the Third Round manager David Booth got the dreaded vote of support from the board only to be shown the door the next week. The scene was now set for the clubs favourite son Chris Turner to lead us to promotion and the fans were not going to be disappointed as a number of our supporters took at two hour journey at Walsall's new ground at Bescott Stadium and returned with 1-0 win thanks to an own goal. Gates were now on the up and the home derby win against the Cobblers just under 6,000 were present Mick Halsall scoring the clincher this sent Northampton Town in to free fall after this result finishing in Tenth position the league at the end of the campaign saw Darlington and Stockport promoted neither still in the Football League.

But the Posh were on auto pilot and went on a thirteen match run undefeated including nine victories and we were up to second place. The manager went a spending spree Ken Charlery and Gary Cooper joining from Maidstone United for £30,000 and Pat Gavin from Leicester City being the notable signings he coming up many vital goals as the run in started. They came to an end against Burnley 4-1 away and two more draws saw us down in fifth place. The next game at home to Cardiff City was sparked by a pitch invasion by their fans don't know why they took a dislike to our players they finished in mid table so could not see the point in can still see Paul Culpin running down the pitch in final minute to slot our third goal in chased by a Cardiff City fan equipped with a Hornell's Milk crate a police dog with his handler in pursuit this added to the goals scored earlier by Des Brenner and David Robinson signed from Newcastle.

We followed this with a 3-0 win with George Berry netting from the spot along with Worrell Stirling and Pat Gavin in front of 7.500 fans. Over 20 coaches went from the Supporters club and many local public houses we were delayed by traffic and police outrider coming adrift from his mighty steed. When some got in us were2-0 down me and Sharon Anne were lucky or unlucky we were in the disabled area and saw it. The win which we needed seamed a mile away a point could take us through if Blackpool lost at Walsall after an hour David Robinson scored with news that Blackpool were losing this spurred the team and 5,000 odd travelling fans the equaliser was perhaps one of the scruffy goals I have seen scored by George Berry courtesy of his afro and Phil Culpins miss kick on the line. With 15 minutes to go we were in poll position Blackpool still losing the game went into slow motion if it had been a boxing match because no action Mr Trussell could had been the first referee to do this. Noel Cantwells apprentice had done the business the crowd invaded the pitch and Posh were in the Third Division taking the team from ninth position to finish fourth. Little did we know that in a seasons time we were going to be promoted again and I was going to see us play at Wembley.

## A SEASON TO REMEMBER.

I am sure to all Posh fans that are old enough to remember this will rate as the top season in the club's history topped by us winning at Wembley. Chris Turner went into the basement for his new signings Marcus Eddon from Everton, Steve Welsh from Cambridge United, Gary Kimble from Gillingham and finally keeper Fred Barber from Walsall for £25,000 who was going to be a cult hero with our fans. The first four games of the 1991/2 season saw us chalk up league wins against Preston North End with a lone David Riley and a 2-1 win at Hull City with goals from Gary Kimble and Ian Mc. Inerney and in the Rumbelows Cup against Aldershot with a Pat Gavin hat trick at home in a 3-1 victory and also scoring along with Mick Halsall at the rural Recreation Ground in the return leg. Then followed a run of six games without a win but included four draws and the end of September was us in the second half of the table.

The second round of the Rumbelows Cup saw us beat a Wimbledon team now playing at a deserted Selhurst Park with goals from Ken Charley and Worrell Stirling. Things were not going as planned and it would be another four games against four league games before we got on track in the league beating Hartlepool's United 3-2 at London Road with David Riley scoring a couple and Ken Charley. In the second leg of the 2nd Round Rumbelows Cup a 2-2 draw against the Dons put us through 4-3 on aggregate Gary Kimble and David Riley scoring. Posh were favoured with a Third Round home draw against Newcastle United and over 10,000 packing the ground to see the Posh win against a struggling team with a late Ken Charley goal.

Fans were now showing their disappointment as to how the season was going after putting in an abysmal display at Shrewsbury when remember Chris Turner coming on the coaches before we left Gay Meadow and apologising for the display. The only good thing about the day was hearing that we had drawn the mighty Liverpool at home if they overcame Port Vale. This spurred the team on with two home wins against Chester City with fewer than 3,000 present in a 2-0 win with goals from Charley. What a difference it was next game as usual all in the city became either Posh fans or Liverpool arm chair fans or is the word followers as vouchers were handed out for the Liverpool game and over 9,000 witnessed a 2-1 victory with David Riley and Worrell Sterling netting. In the F.A. Cup 1st Round we made short work of non league Harlow Town to the tune of 7-0. The game on the Saturday before the main event saw only just over 4,000 draw with Torquay United with Paul Culpin netting for us. On the Tuesday night 14,000 fans packed London Road to see one more great cup epics against an in form Reds and really took the game to them from the off and came as no surprise when Gary Kimble gave us a 19th minute lead with a miss hit cross in my opinion he will tell you otherwise from Noel Luke pass Bruce Grobelaar made a pigs ear of it and Kimble said thank you very much to send the Posh fans in raptures.

Could we hang on for 70 minutes? We did and had to thank Fred Barber's late great save to see us through to another chapter. Back to the F.A. Cup on the Saturday at home to Reading and a goalless draw and going down 1-0 in the replay. We were still mid table in the Division a home win 3-0 against Hull City watched by many fans attending to get vouchers for the next round at the Rumbelows Cup yes the Quarter final against Middlesbrough going well in Division Two and they finished runners up and went up into the new Premiership at the end of the campaign. Two good away draws a 3-3 cracker against Stoke City with Mick Halsall, David Robinson and Worrell Stirling scoring, then a 1-1 draw at Preston North End on their plastic pitch which to me was a farce the bounce was so high that the keepers Fred Barber for us and think it was Alan Kelly for them had their own game and looked the most likely scorers but Ken Charlery did get one under the cross bar.

The Middlesbrough game again saw a bumper gate but produced no goals. By the time the replay mainly due to the replay being called off very late think we had at least 15 coaches and we were turned back by the law at Hartshead Moor services as referee Ken Hackett called it off and previously we had the aborted trip to Mansfield Town in the Autoglass Trophy called off for fog with us losing 2-1 the team were now in the top half of the table. The club I think I am right in saying the club paid for the coaches to go back for the re arranged game at Ayersome Park the tie being settled by Stuart Ripley lone goal.

Posh were moving up the table well despite because of replays were now in action twice a week moving on now in the Autoglass Trophy with a lone Peter Costello goal at home to Shrewsbury Town this was included in a ten match victory run along with the defeat of Exeter City in the Second round beating former giants like Fulham, Bolton Wanderers and Huddersfield in the run. Even the award of Manager of the Month did not put the usual kiss of death on the team. Little did we know at the end of the season that the Terriers were going to play a part in the club's history?

Remember well the trip to Bournemouth apart from a 2-0 victory with

Bobby Barnes and Dave Riley scoring we were perhaps first in the ground when I saw a £10 note on the floor told Sharon to put her foot on it as she was in her wheelchair and it was a good day all round. After the win against Wrexham in the Area Semi Final of the Autoglass at home 3-1 our run came to an abrupt half win no win in the next five games and we fell out of the promotion frame. Ian Bennett was thrust into the limelight making his Posh debut in the Autoglass Trophy Southern Area Final and things did not go to plan Stoke City racing into a 2-0 lead with in five minutes and the nearly 15,000 crowd belting out Delilah Break Down the door but the Posh battled back to earn a 3-3 draw with goals from Mick Halsall, Ken Charley and an own goal.

Could we get to Wembley on two fronts as the goalless home draw saw us up to seventh with a game in hand? The return leg of the Autoglass was made all ticket and we missed out in an ugly game by a lone goal scored by Paul Ware. Now it was back to the promotion trail two wins and two draws and my mate Gary Cooper going absent without leave and missing out on a day at Wembley. The end of the season saw two long journeys drawing 2-2 at Exeter City with goals from Ken Charley and Whittlesey youngster Gary Butterworth which please Sharon Anne as another one of her favourite players then followed by the 520 round trip for our last away game at Torquay United again a 2-2 draw with Ken Charley scoring both goals but the point was not enough to see us in the Play Off Semi Finals. All kinds of permutations were hanging over the last home game against leaders Brentford who won and were crowned champions with alone Gary Blisset goal but both camps were happy as the other results went well us and we were in the Play Offs against Huddersfield Town where my Posh Affair nearly started could the little Posh be playing at Wembley?

First leg was at London Road and the Terriers took an lead after half an hour but it took only seconds after the break for Ken Charley to level but David Robinson cleared into his own net to put them ahead we were under tremendous pressure but a great three man move saw Mick Halsall level in the dying minutes to sent the Posh fans in the nearly 12,000 crowd home with a hope of appearing at Wembley and could they get time off to witness one of the greatest games in the club's history.

Over 3,500 followed the club on the 250 mile round trip on a midweek evening our hopes were dashed with a second minute Terriers goal by Chris Billy and hung on till the break still fortunate to only be a goal behind. Whatever Chris Turner said to them at the break they came out a different outfit. Worrell Stirling took on the giant keeper for a race for the ball nicked it by him into the net and was orbited into next week and was soon replaced with Steve Cooper in an end to end game but with four minutes our dreams were reality with Steve Cooper scoring a diving header and into Posh history and to Wembley for the first time poor Steve passed away only aged 39 in 2004 in his sleep with a cracked skull from a fall.

For me and I know for Sharon Anne and lots of fans this was perhaps the best memory how long our players spent celebrating felt sorry for them all they wanted to do was get home we could not careless the result of the other Semi Final gave us a final against Stockport County in our 67th game of the season. Sunday 24th May saw the city deserted as nearly 25,000 fans travelled to Wembley as against the 10,000 of Stockport County Fred Barber came out in his usual mask and for the warm up. Think we had about 30 odd coaches which we brought in from all over the region they were treated to an end to end first half but remained goalless until a very controversial goal a Ken Charley header hitting the underside of the bar and bouncing over the line and Martin Boddenham the referee on consulting his linesman gave the goal spoke to him about it a couple of years ago as he was Umpiring at Trent Bridge he remembered it well. County thought they were on level terms as the giant Kevin Francis netted but was struck off for offside. Disaster struck with four minutes to go an Andy Preece cross was not cup out by Fred Barber and Kevin Francis headed home. But in the last minute Marcus Ebdon set up Ken Charley to lop the ball over Neil Edwards five foot eight frame to send the Posh fans into extersy the final whistle went four minutes later and Posh were in the second tier of English football the new First Division. Skipper Mick Halsall collected the trophy shaped like a Barclays Eagle the wear about is not known often asked about it by older fans on my tours me and my mate Bob Burrows are always searching E bay for it. My dad was not in good health and made the journey this was to be his last match blesses him supporting the club passing away in Sue Ryder Thorpe Hall in June 1993 leaving me to carry on my POSH AFFAIR. The long season over the next day the team toured the city starting from the Marriot where Fred Barber gave Sharon Anne his warm up jersey and his gloves and then they all went in the city to be greeted by the fans on the balcony at the Town Hall.

**IN WITH THE BIG BOYS**

Chris Turner kept faith in his squad the only signing in the summer of 1992/3 season being Darren Bradshaw from Newcastle United as the club were now in the First Division with the Premier League coming into being leaping from the old League 3 Biggest disappointment about the opening home game against Derby County was when just under 10,000 saw Ken Charley net the only goal this was enhanced by a big Rams following. Seemed that nearly 20,000 that made the Wembley trip had forgot where London Road was already. The season started well the first defeat coming after six games including two legs win against Barnet. First defeat came in a ding dong battle at Wolverhampton Wanderers despite goals from Mick Halsall, Ken Charley and Worrell Stirling returned empty handed on a 4-3 defeat.

Things were not good off the pitch with club Chairman wanting to sell the club because of failing health and two of last season's heroes leaving Ken Charley to Watford for £350,000 and Dave Robinson to Nott's County for £450,000 which was a good deal for the club but not for Dave as knee injury brought his career to an end after only a couple of games for the County although we brought in for £85,000 Tony Philliskirk from Bolton Wanderers and Dominic Iorfa from Galastasary who was to be a cult hero in his short career at the club. It was rumoured that a little fat man who swears a lot was interested in buying the club with a few mates from Barnet namely Barry Fry, Mr Devaney said they could have it if they could raise two million pounds. One win in six games saw the club just above halfway and knocked out of the League Cup by Leicester City but the tables were turned when we beat they in league 2-0 at Filbert Street with Tony Philliskirk scoring his first Posh goal and Worrell Stirling Philliskirk went one better scoring twice at Watford in a 2-1 win in a the Watford was the man he replaced Ken Charley. One of the best home games of the season was the demolition of Sunderland 5-2 with a goal glut of three goals in four minutes Tony Adcock gave us an early lead then scored a second with Gary Cooper, Tony Philliskirk and Dominic Iorfa netting. Posh were in trouble with the FA again this time in the First round replay against non league Kingstonians, Tony Adcock goal brought the tie back to London Road Posh showed them no mercy and romped into a 3-0 lead when an idiot in the London Road end threw a 50p coin which hit the keeper on the head leading to him being taken off and Posh finished the job 9-1 with Tony Philliskirk netting five times a club record or he thought, two from Tony Adcock, Gary Cooper and an own goal and one of the best goals of the game scored by our opponents.

The F.A. ordered a replay behind closed doors and the culprit was never caught and Posh won 1-0 with a Worrell Stirling goal in front of an official attendance of none. The 2nd Round of the Cup saw us get the dreaded draw the great trek to Plymouth Argyle a long journey home on a 3-2 defeat with goals from Tony Philliskirk and Worrell Stirling not being enough. Finally the future of the club was assured when Chris Turner assembled a consortium to buy the club off John Devaney and he became Chairman and his assistant Lil Fucillo stepped up to the managers role Chris going from club captain to chairman. The game away to Bristol City was a milestone for popular player Steve Welsh he scored his first goal for the club a toe ender or a volley one of his two he even scored in his whole career in a 1-0 victory and what a celebration it was. Posh had gone six games unbeaten at London Road but the disappointment was five were draws and by the end of 1992 we were in 13th position and we after falling to three defeats against tough opponents Newcastle United, Birmingham City will remember that one because my Sharon Anne had a spat with Karen Brady all tarter up although with Sharon Anne she was up at the crack of dawn putting on her make up for an away trip remember her nearly knocking me out with hair spray in the bathroom before a trip to Luton one season, and at Millwall not scoring a single goal in all the games perhaps one of the best wins of the season was the 3-2 win away to Derby County.

We now had the ranks swelled with signings of John McGlashan from Milwall for £100,000 and Tony Psycho Spearing from Plymouth Argyle fighting back from a two nil deficits with goals from Andy Curtis, Tony Philliskirk and Tony Adcock. Followed again by three defeats then three wins on the trot against Brentford, Grimsby Town and Birmingham City put us in the top ten in the First Division. Even though we went on a seven run winless run with only draws against Cambridge United at the Abbey Stadium, home draws against Oxford United and Watford. The Wembley team was starting to break up Mick Halsall had a bad injury which was later to end his career and Noel Luke Doris as we all knew him was to leave after 336 games for the club now working with me on match days we joke only six good games among them a great servant to the club but don't ask him about Chris Turner say no more.

The run in to the end of the season resulted in just one defeat in the last seven games including the 3-0 defeat of Leicester City at London Road in front of over 15,000 fans at home the best gate of the season with goals from Tony Philliskirk, Tony Adcock and Marcus Ebdon another player like Tommy Robson who would not survive in today's game Tommy with his diving and Marcus with his two footed tackles and despite the last two games being draws the Posh finished in 10th place the highest position then and still today in its league history. Perhaps our downfall was lack of goals only netting 55 times Tony Adcock top of the pile with 16 goals but a season to remember for the fans

## AFTER THE LORD MAYOR'S SHOW

Season 1993/4 was going to be season that was going to be a complete contrast to the previous one with popular players shown the door Worrell Stirling moving to Bristol Rovers for £140,000 and Ronnie Robinson to Exeter City and signed full back David McDonald from Tottenham, Mark Peters from Norwich and Jason Brissett from Arsenal all on free transfers and as the season went by you could see why and in my opinion we signed lots of players like this in the season to help survive in the Championship. First match was at Leicester City as they were behind with completing the new away stand Posh fans were not allowed to attend. Good old Jenny Brown to the rescue she had friends in Leicester and she managed to get tickets for me and Sharon Anne we were spotted by our Police Sergeant John Harlock he nodded and said good afternoon and we were in but Sharon Anne forgot herself when Gary Cooper scored our end from the spot but that was not enough and we lost 2-1.

After three games we were fifth with a 4-1 win over Barnsley and a draw at home to Nott's County where Steve Welsh scored his other Posh career goal. But then the free fall began a 3-1 win at home was something for the fans to get excited about with Tony Philliskirk netting a hat trick but four games without a victory saw us in the basement area. But away from the league troubles we had a good run in the League Cup beating Barnsley, Blackpool before going out after a replay away to Portsmouth. We were in a rush to turn things around signing not Ian but David Rush from Sunderland his stay was brief as we could not afford him. Our friend Gary Cooper left to join Barry Fry at Birmingham City for a free good bit of dealing by the Little Fat Man also joining Ian Bennett who he paid £325,000 for Ken Charley came the other way back to London Road for £170,000. With us not coming in till Round Three in the FA cup our stay was brief a draw 1-1 at home to Tottenham Hotspurs with Jason Brissett netting before a late equaliser took the game back to White Hart Lane between the replay we beat W.B.A at home 2-0 with own goal and Ken Charley netting must have been a massive following from London as the attendance for this game was seven thousand odd and the Cup Match again at home over 19,000.

The trip to London was heartbreak for local youngster Andy Furnell bravely electing to take a spot kick after extra time and missing and we went out 5-4 on spot kicks this only his second game for the club. Andy is still on the local football scene as coach for The Cuckoos Yaxley F.C. in the Premier League of the United Counties League. Previous to this Lil Fucillo called it a day and resigned Alf Hand was asked by Chris Turner to take over the Chairman's duties and him to take over the team duties. We managed to get off the bottom with a home win against Middlesbrough with a lone Ken Charlery strike and even rose to 21st with wins against Southend United, Oxford United and a home draw against Derby County with Ken Charlery and Dominic Iorfa scoring he became a cult hero in his short spell at the club scoring some great goals but often wanted a bigger pitch or forgot to take the ball with him his son of the same name is now carving a career at Wolves.

The Millwall game which we lost by an own goal by Chris Greenman who Sharon Anne was friends with was painful for her as she was ribbed about it all the way home and then he spent the night on our sofa. The season ended painfully after this game we only picked up from the last ten games a mere two points but we had some good games losing 4-3 at home to Watford a draw at Wolves and the 3-2 defeat against Nottingham Forest in front of 14,000 at home but still remember Scott Cooksey's debut in goal against Charlton Athletic a 5-1 defeat surprisingly he went on to make 20 appearances for the club. At this game a bald smart gentleman set next to us asking us about players it turned out to be our next manager John Still. The season ended with us finishing bottom of the pile and back to Division Two with a 4-1 defeat at Bristol City. During the close season after retiring from a very successful veteran running career as a tribute to Sue Ryder Home Thorpe Hall for looking after my father Walter I with Richard Luxford my back up man walked all round the homes in East Anglia raising about £5,000 with a big donation from my employer Freemans P.L.C. a journey of about 300 miles and was honoured to have breakfast with Lady Ryder of Warsaw on her birthday at the Sue Ryder Headquarters at Cavendish in Suffolk. My delight was tainted when soon after Sharon Anne was diagnosed as having Lupus.

**STILL HOPING**

Who is John Still the Posh fans must have asked when appointed in 1994/5 season as he had never managed in the Football League but had lots of success on the non league circuit. During the season we had a very busy revolving door at the club. Of the promotion team both Fred Barber and Tony Adcock went to Luton Town and Lee Howarth to Mansfield and seven other players released on free transfers. Big money was paid for big Sean Farrell £120,000 from Fulham, along with centre half Gary Breen from Gillingham for £70,000 and smaller fees for Greg Heald and David Morrison from non league teams and also some frees. Posh got off the mark in the third game beating Brentford away with a lone Ken

Charlery goal the then were thrashed 5-1 at home by Crewe Alexander.

One of the players the fans did not warm to was keeper Scott Cooksey his error losing points at Shrewsbury but Posh were on a reasonable run beating Hull City 2-1 at home with goals from David Morrison and Ken Charlery and now in seventh spot. A comical error by Scott Cooksey at Huddersfield Town trying to dribble the ball and costing a goal was the last straw for the manager and he was dropped for Mark Tyler for the Birmingham City game which was shown on Sky or maybe it was ITV the Blues putting three past him in the first half hour finally winning 4-0 not a good start for the seventeen year old now waiting for his S.A.G.A. holiday books being delivered now he is forty this game first in a Posh shirt and a record number of appearances only beaten by Tommy Robson he did retain his place for the next two games once again Birmingham City went one goal better putting five past him in a 5-3 defeat in the Auto Windscreens Shield then John Still brought in Mark Prudhoe from Stoke City on loan Posh were having a strange season not being able to win at London Road only one win in nine tries and we were in the bottom half of the table.

For once we kept a clean sheet with a 1-0 win at Plymouth Argyle with Leburd Henry scoring little did the Mrs know that me and Sharon Anne were sponsoring his track suit. Mark Prudhoes stay was brief fans wishing he would sign two wins against Chester City in the league and Walsall in the Auto Windowscreens Shield was overshadowed by the game away to Brighton and Hove Albion Posh winning the game with nine men with Ken Charlery and David Morrison being sent off with goals from Ken Charlery before he left the field and Marcus Ebdon it was like we had won the National Lottery on the first night of it coming into being. In the First Round of the F.A. Cup we knocked out Northampton Town at home 4-0 with Ken Charlery netting twice, Lee Williams and Leburd Henry but went out in the Second Round at home to Cambridge United 2-0.

Results were poor we went on a fourteen game winless run drawing six and struggling in 18th position. Can remember going to Hereford on a bitter November night perhaps only a couple of dozen on the coach we lost 2-0 and David Morrison who had made the journey but left out moaning about having to get up in the morning for think it was a Reserve game in the afternoon told him what I thought of him me having to get up at six for work in the morning. Another keeper arrived Fred Barber back on loan quickly followed by the fifth of the season John Keeley on a free from somewhere he soon departed shipping ten goals in three games can remember him being pelted with a pie at one of games what a waste of a pie he was awful.

Now we had a giant 6ft-7in American keeper from West Ham Ian Feuer and the contrasting tiny Billy Manuel signed on loan from Cambridge United. We went on an unbeaten run of four draws but only one victory, things were now looking up and we kept our distance from the re election zone and after losing 3-1 at Wycombe Wanderers two victories against Huddersfield Town our old foes upsetting their playoff hopes with Brian McGorry and Marcus Ebdon scoring and the bulky Tony Kelly netting from the spot to claim a 1-0 victory at home to Swansea City we lost to local rivals Cambridge United at the Abbey 2-0 then home wins against Wrexham, Blackpool and draws against Stockport County and York City saw us finish safely in 15th position. Even in a very poor season the fans kept faith and the average attendance were just over 5,000.

The new season 1995/6 saw John Still in charge but now supported by former skipper the popular Mick Halsall who had to retire in the last season through injury the fans were upset when Ken Charley was sold to Barry Fry at Birmingham City for £350,000 again money would have been tight. But they soon added Lee Power now the Chairman at Swindon Town from Norwich City for £80,000 and £150,000 for keeper Jon Sheffield from Cambridge United plus a host of free transfers coming and going. Can remember walking alongside Chris Turner, with thousands of fans to lobby the Peterborough City Council for permission to build a new 5,000 capacity stand on the Glebe Road stand which was passed so we played on a three sided ground for most of the season fans and management seeming to be getting on well.

Day one in the season we were top with a 3-1 win at home to Brighton and Hove Albion with Simon Clark, Sean Farrell and new signing Gary Martindale scoring but it was to be another eight games before another one apart from beating Swansea City in the Football League Cup going through 3-0 in extra time after losing 4-1 at Vetch Field in first leg Nightmare draw in the Auto Winderscreen Trophy away to Plymouth Argyle but we progressed with a 3-0 win with Simon Clark, Lee Power and Scott McGleish netting but then were on a 5-1 defeat against Rotherham at Millmoor. In the two legged Football League Cup we were trashed by Aston Villa 6-0 at Villa Park but drew the meaningless second leg 1-1 with Gary Martindale the scorer. The 3-0 defeat at Brentford saw John Stills reign as manager come to an end after a season and a half and the club and leaving with us in 17th place. Nice bloke always has a chat if he comes to a game and a very successful manager at lower league level but not at Posh.

Now the job was passed over to Mick Halsall and what a start could not believe what we were seeing Posh stormed into a first half three goal lead and added the same second half with two goals each from Garry Martindale, David

Morrison and others from Arsenal loan player Paul Shaw and Lee Power at home against York City. Then we went on a six game unbeaten run with a lone Neil Le Bihan goal think it was direct from a corner in the First Round of the F.A. Cup at Exeter City a win in the AutoWindow Screens Shield with the new Golden Goal Rule with Sean Farrell netting the important goal. Followed by a 4-0 win in the Second round of the F.A. Cup non league Bognor Regis Town were sent packing 4-0 with a Sean Farrell hat trick and Marcus Ebdon. In the Cup games we were doing well in again in Round Three saw off Wrexham at home with Neil Le Bihan scoring the only goal and in the mid week after beating Colchester United 3-2 in the Auto Windowscreens Shield with goals from a brace from Gary Martindale and Scott McGleish another player who was very successful as a scorer in his long league career but not at London Road.

A ding dong battle against Bournemouth saw us on a 5-4 loss with Sean Farrell and Gary Martindale scoring a couple each followed by a 2-1 victory at Brighton and Hove Albion with Paul Shaw a very good loan signing who we could not afford nothing changes from Arsenal scoring both goals. The revolving door kept turning bringing back Ken Charlery for a fee no doubt Barry Fry negotiated from Birmingham City not knowing he would be one of his players again next campaign Gary Breen moved to the Blues for £240,000 and we signed Marc Foran to replace him not much of a swap. We went out of the F.A. Cup in Round Four away at Huddersfield Town 2-0 and in the A.W.S in the Area Semi Final 1-0 home to Bristol Rovers. Only just over 4,000 fans saw the humbling of Carlisle United at home to the tune of 6-1 and Posh now in 18th place our scorers were Ken Charlery and Sean Farrell two each, Marcus Ebdon and Gary Martindale his last game before joining Nott's County with a good scoring record a goal well under three games for us. We brought in cheap replacements and then paid £225,000 for Carl Griffith a club record he scored with his first kick in his debut a 3-2 loss to Walsall at home that's the only think he will be remembered for. A terrible run of only one win in the twelve last games a 3-1 win at home to Hull City with Lee Power. Sean Farrell and Ken Charlery netting in front of a crowd of over 6,600 a result to be expected as they finished bottom nine points adrift. Last two games we lost both away to Crewe Alexandra and Oxford United and finished another season of turmoil and just out of the drop zone in 19th position.

## BAZZA FRYS IN

Days after the end of the season and well before the start of 1996/7 season a little fat man was named as manager and fortunately it was not Adi Mowles it was

Barry Fry who a few years earlier was linked with the Posh but this was going to be a roller coaster of a season for Fry after being sacked at the end of the last season by the Blues. He spent out on a club record signing £350,000 for Martin O; Connor from Walsall, Mick Bodley from the Blues for £75,000 and fans were elated when Steve Welsh returned from Partick Thistle for £58,000 along with several free transfers from Barry Fry's former clubs. It was not clear if Barry Fry had come to take over the club but the fans backed him with good season ticket sales. On the playing staff he still had Lil Fucillo on his along with Mick Halsall as his coach and brought his old mate Gordon Ogbourne who had served him at many clubs as his kit man in.

The season started with a lone goal defeat at Bristol Rovers and we could not find the net losing by the lone goal in the first leg of the Football League Cup against Milwall. Now I in a new job and not so easy to get time off for night matches and if could not have half days holiday had to miss some away journeys and by now my dear Sharon Anne had found other interests on a Saturday. We managed to overcome Millwall in the second leg of the Football League Cup winning 2-0 at London Road after extra time with strikes from Ken Charley and Carl Griffiths. The next four games did bring a victory but unlucky when Milwall levelled in the last minute in a 3-3 draw at London Road with Zeke Rowe, Ken Charley and Martin O, Connor scoring. We made the long journey to Southampton in the Second Round of the League even longer coming home as we lost 2-0 and they finished us off a week later to the tune of 4-1 Sean Farrell scoring for us. Most entertaining of the season so far was the 6-3 home defeat of Wycombe Wanderers and a draw at Plymouth Argyle and another exciting win at Preston North End 4-3 Simon Clark, Scott Houghton, Ken Charley and Zeke Rowe the scorers coming back from 3-1 down it seemed that Barry Fry's policy was that if not matter how many you score we will score more and it certainly was good on the eye and good value for the fans. Then the wheels came off with us in mid table the next ten games only one win in the next eleven league games but we did manage to knock Cheltenham Town out of the First Round of the F.A Cup with two extra time from Ken Charley to add to his earlier one and Giuliano Grazioli seeing the Posh through 3-1.

During this run a bombshell was announced in the local press that Barry Fry did not own the club and they were at least two and a half million pounds in debt. This meant that the club disposed of the services of Lil Fucillo and Mick Halsall and started a fire sale of players Martin O'Connor being the first going to Birmingham for £500,000 and Andy Edwards coming in exchange. The gloom was lifted for a while with the 6-2 win at home to Rotherham United with Martin Carruthers a £75,000 signing from Stoke City netting twice along with Roger Willis, Scott Houghton and an own goal. Second Round of the F.A. Cup saw us beat another non league side Enfield but after a draw away beating them 4-1 in the return with Martin Carruthers scoring another brace and wins at home to home to Burnley with Carruthers a couple with David Morrison netting then next game at 2-0 win at Milwall with Scott Houghton striking twice big deal we were out of the relegation zone. The long trek to Plymouth Argyle saw us progress past the F.A. Cup third round with Ken Charley netting the lone goal of the game then we had an aborted away game to Wycombe Wanderers a game that never should have started on an icy surface but we did get a glance of another Posh Legend to be David Farrell was in the hosts team we were losing 2-0 at the time.

We were progressing well A.W.S. beating Walsall at home 2-0 at home in the Second Round and then the Area Quarter Final beating Exeter City away by a single goal. Wrexham did the double over us with wins firstly at home in the Fourth Round of the F.A. winning 4-2 and a couple of weeks later 1-0 on the back of a 5-1 hiding at Blackpool. Another of Barry Fry's old players from Birmingham City was signed Ricky Otto on loan scored the only goal that saw us see off Watford in the A.W,S Area Semi Final then scoring the goal in a 1-1 draw home to Chesterfield draw were down in 22nd place and another trashing followed at Burnley. Now we were in the Area Final of the A.W.S a two leg game against Colchester United and dreams of another day out at Wembley and welcome cash for the club as relegation was on the horizon. The first leg at home was Posh take a healthy 2-0 lead with Ricky Otto and Ken Charley strikes back to the ramshackle Layer Road but the trip was not to be with Ken Charley being sent off by showman referee Uriah Rennie and Bart Griemink having one of his many bad days in goal at we lost 3-0 the game ending with a golden goal.

Barry Fry now appointed Phil Neal the old England defender as his number two results did not improve can still see Aidy Boothroyd writhing in agony on the ground with his arm up a broken leg ended his career in a goalless draw at Notts. County. Ken Charley scored in his last appearance for the club in the 1-1 draw at Crewe Alexandra a player that will always be remember in Posh fans hearts and is in the Posh Hall of Fame strangely joining Stockport County after breaking the fans hearts at Wembley for £75,000. Marcus Ebdon went to Chesterfield the last of the Wembley team for £100,000. We spent some of the money on defender Des Linton and striker Miguel De Souza. Barry Fry brought a windfall for the club selling youth stars Dave Billington and Mark McKeever for a £1,000,000 to Sheffield Wednesday after only handfuls of games between them sadly their careers did not take off Dave Billington received an injury that ended his short career. With six games to go we saw off Bournemouth at home 3-1 saw us still in 22nd position despite goals from Simon Clark, Miguel De Souza and Ricky Otto next game was vital against York City down at the bottom like us and we lost by a single goal a win at Preston North End with Roger Willis and Miguel De Souza scoring loses against Bury and home defeat to promotion chasing Luton Town in front of over 9,000 fans the best of the season. Last game of the season Posh fielded Matthew Etherington became the youngest player to play for Posh at 15 years and 262 Adam Drury scored for us and we survived in 22nd place. In a disastrous season players had been sold to balance the books and we had used 44 players. Then followed the television programme there's Only One Barry Fry which was not a good advert for the club after a season to forget. One of the pleasing facts that the gates had gone up over nearly 500 averages but how they had suffered

The fans were hoping that Barry Fry's second season was going to be better than his first what was 1997/8 going to bring. Several players arrived among them David Farrell from Wycombe Wanderers Steve Castle from Leyton Orient and veteran striker Jimmy Quinn from Reading and Simon Clark Greg Heald, Jon Sheffield and Roger Willis going the other way. Season started with a 1-0 defeat at home to Scunthorpe United beating Portsmouth over two legs in the Football League Cup with David Farrell scoring his first goal for the club at Fratton Park. We then went on a eleven game unbeaten run the highlights being the 5-0 away defeat against a very poor Doncaster Rovers side with Martin Carruthers netting a pair and at home to Barnet 5-0 with Jimmy Quinn scoring a hat trick. The run ended with a 2-1 defeat at Hartlepool's United and we were knocked off top spot. We were now becoming draw specialists but along with three wins against Torquay United our neighbours Cambridge United 1-0 with Jimmy Quinn netting with over 10,000 present at London Road and after losing 2-0 to Reading in the Football League Cup at second hurdle. In the F.A. Cup we made progress beating Swansea City 4-1 at Vetch Field with Steve Castle netting twice plus Jimmy Quinn and Martin Carruthers and in the Second Round beating non league Dagenham and Redbridge 3-2 with goals from Jimmy Quinn two one a late winner and Martin Carruthers.

Lincoln City going well in the division were knocked back by a great first half performance Posh being 4-1 up at the break with David Farrell and Martin Carruthers each scoring twice aided by an own goal winning 5-1 again in front of a bumper 8,000 gate. We had our usual Christmas form and our run came to an end on Boxing Day at Barnet losing 2-0 and then two days later at home to Brighton and Hove Albion despite Jimmy Quinn scoring losing 2-1 in front of a healthy holiday crowd Posh being reduced to ten men with Ashley Vickers being shown the red card on his debut for the club he never played for the club again. Not many fans turned out for the A.W.S. then we played Swansea City just over a thousand and we progressed to Round Three with a 2-1 win. Walsall ended our F.A. Cup run at home 2-0 in front of over of nearly 13,000 fans with the carrot being a trip to Old Trafford but it was not to be.

Form was now getting a worry although still in second place but the defeat by Doncaster Rovers at home got the alarm bells ringing a last minute goal gave them only their third win of the season they only managed 20 points all season. We went out of the A.W.S. after beating Northampton Town in Round we again went out to Walsall once again in the Area Semi Final and then we went on a terrible run from the Rotherham game at home winning by a lone Jimmy Quinn strike we went nine games without winning including Doncaster Rovers doing the double over us and we had fallen to eighth position. It ended with a 2-1 win home to Chester City with Martin Carruthers and David Farrell scoring. In barren spell Barry Fry sacked Phil Neal and this was not a popular choice with Posh fans being the fifth one disposed of in his two years as manager. A home win 1-0 at home to Nott's County perhaps gave us a bit of hope then followed by a 1-0 defeat at Cambridge United who wanted to charge me £10 for every coach that we parked on Coldhams Common and we about ten very rude reply and I did not pay. Last four games we only picked up one win home to Cardiff City 2-0 with Nial Inman and Steve Castle on target and the season petered out with two defeats against Lincoln City and Torquay United with the fans staging a protest for Barry Fry to go in a season that that promised so much at Christmas time but produced nothing at the end last game of the campaign was goalless against Hartlepool's United and we finished in 10th place but despite this Jimmy Quinn who netted 20 league goals, Scott Houghton and David Farrell were elected in the P.F.A. Third Division team of the season. Barry Fry was not a popular figure and the natives were not happy.

**NEARLY A PERFECT TEN**

Barry Fry was still manager getting backing from now new Chairman Peter Boizot of Pizza Express fame. Not much money was spent on new arrivals the only one being Richard Scott from Shrewsbury Town. The season 1998/9 produced no victories against English sides in friendlies and the first league game was a 1-0 defeat at home to Halifax. One the best ever players produced from our Youth Academy in my eyes Simon Davies was to make his entrance in the Football League Cup First Leg at Reading in a 1-1 draw with Martin Carruthers netting. First victory came at Cardiff City's Ninian Park where the person opening the Main Gate looked like he had come from the Adams family and you could see the rats feeding under a burger van winning 3-1 with two goals from new loan player Leon McKenzie from Crystal Palace and Martin Carruthers. We soon went out of the Football League Cup losing the second leg at home to Reading 2-0. We warmed up for the Barnet rout with a 4-1 home defeat of Exeter City with goals from Jimmy Quinn two, Leon McKenzie and Andy Edwards.

Poor old John Still was in charge at Barnet and they had several ex Posh players in their ranks the day started bad for the hosts with a player sent off within ten minutes and by half time we had raced into a 4-1 lead we ever scored the Bees goal Mick Bodley scoring the wrong end they had another player sent off and finished up on a 9-1 mauling with Guliano Grazioli netting five a club record, Jimmy Quinn a couple, Dean Hooper and Matthew Etheringtons first goal for the club past Nicky Rust think he was making his debut for the Bees after a long career at Brighton Hove Albion. Next game we raced into a three goal lead before the break against Chester City that being the final score line with Guliano Grazioli, Scott Houghton and Simon Davis netting but the result was tinged with sadness as the news was that Jimmy Quinn was leaving to return to management with Swindon Town a big blow for the club as in his 47 league games he had started he had netted 25 times. One good signing on paper was Phil Chapple ex Cambridge United and Charlton Athletic but he only managed to appear 17 times in his Posh career and retired with a back injury but remained with the club till 2003 in coaching roles. To make thinks even worse Crystal Palace recalled Leon McKenzie as we could not afford his fee. The Barnet result was soon forgot nine games only brought in two wins against Hartlepool's United away 2-0 with a Martin Carruthers goal and a grass cutter from Richard Scott netting think this might have been the first year we met the old man who dressed up as a lady he looked grotesque with his hairy legs and high heels he always went to the away end and a few of our supporters stood outside the gents till he came out is that right Lenny you were one of them.

Another flop was the signing of Sam Allardyces son Craig hopes him a better agent than he was player only managing a handful of games but we had also signed the popular defender Andy Legge. Had we turned the corner when we beat rivals Cambridge United at London Road 2-1 in front of a bumper crowd of over 10,000 with us going well and getting promoted at the end of the campaign goals from Steve Castle and Leon McKenzie back again? Used to tell people, jokingly that when my namesake Drewe Broughton joined the club that he was my son. Early exit from the F.A.Cup fell at the first fence to a late goal at Wrexham then went on a run of only one defeat in six including a win in the A.W.S. against Leyton Orient who we played again in the league this time at Brisbane Road four days later winning 2-1 with Drewe Broughton and Leon McKenzie netting. The 3-1 win at Scarborough's McCain Stadium at Seamer now the only thing standing was the Main Gate when was a holiday a couple of years ago took us to fifth place with David Farrell, Andy Edwards and Leon McKenzie strikes.

Next eight games including going out of the A.W.S. to Bournemouth to the tune of 5-1 away we only won once that was at home to Cardiff City 2-1 with goals from Steve Castle and Guliano Grazioli and we fell to mid table. Barnet were the whipping boys again when the slump ended with us trailing 2-1 at the break a new loan striker from Wayne Andrews completed a hat trick inside ten minutes and added a late fourth goal to see Posh win 5-2. Form did not return and the only win in seven games was the long journey to Plymouth Argyle winning 2-0 goals coming from Wayne Andrews and Drew Broughtons backside as he charged down a Jon Sheffield clearance now playing for the Pilgrims. Two wins on the bounce gave us a bit of hope beating Mansfield a lone David Farrell giving us a home win and then a 3-0 away win at Rochdale with Guliano Grazioli scoring a couple and Simon Davies with seven games to go it looked as though another in Division Three was nigh and the last seven games only brought two wins at home to Torquay United 4-0 with Guliano Grazioli netting, Matthew Etherington, Dean Hooper and Francis Green and another home win against Leyton Orient 3-0 with Dave Farrell, Guliano Grazioli scoring his last Posh goal being given a free transfer in the summer despite being top scorer with 15 goals and Drewe Broughton.

The final game of the season meant nothing to the Posh but for poor old Scarborough their world collapsed thinking that they had survived after drawing 1-1 with us and prematurely celebrating the news came through that the Carlisle keeper Jimmy Glass had come up for a corner in added time and scored and Scarborough were out off the Football league after a league career that had lasted twelve years with Posh finishing ninth Barry Frys magic had failed once again but read on.

**A WEMBLEY RETURN.**

As usual not much to look forward no money the only arrival being Andy Clarke from Wimbledon had a long career with them but his 170 games only yielded 17 goals he arrived on a free but he was to be a hero for the Posh. Seven players were shown the door and we put faith in the likes of youngsters Matthew Etherington and Simon Davies. Season started well with a 2-1 win at home to Hartlepool's united with Steve Castle and Francis Green netting then a great win at Sixfields in front of a healthy crowd of over 6,000 with Simon Davies scoring the only goals. Our run in the Football League Cup we fell at the first hurdle going out to Reading 2-1 on aggregate.

Barry Fry then spent the biggest mistake in my opinion in all my years of watching the club when he signed Howard Forrinton from his old club Birmingham City for £250,000 mainly because Andy Clarke was struggling with injury. Home form not like today's was very good as up end of November and defeat at home to Barnet we had gone seven wins and a draw but again we went out of the F.A. in the First Round after a replay at Brighton and Hove Albion now playing at Withdean Athletic Stadium in a posh part of Brighton were the local council would not allow music to be played only Sussex by the sea on match days and you needed to have a pair of binoculars to see what was happening on the pitch and players came out over a bridge built up over the athletic track nothing was to our liking and we suffered a 3-0 defeat. The game before this saw us go top of the pile with a 4-1 win at home to Shrewsbury Town with now fit again Andy Clarke netting twice, Steve Castle and Howard Forrinton. But then we had an alarming drop of form after the Barnet defeat at Hartlepool's United 1-0 were got talking to local bobby and he said I used to play for the Posh and it was Eric Young who joined on loan from Manchester United on loan a classy midfield player made 25 appearances for us scoring twice in 1972-3 season, small world.

Rotherham did not bring us any Christmas cheer thrashing us 5-0 at home another win and a draw and a win at Hull City 3-2 with Andy Clarke striking twice and Richard Scott saw us down to mid table The fans were not happy as youngsters Simon Davies and Matthew Etherington were sold to Tottenham Hotspurs for combined total of £1.2 million. Out in the First Round of A.W.S 1-0 home to Brentford then new signing Jason Lee signed from Nottingham Forest netted the only goal at home to Northampton Town and then again in the 1-1 draw at Leyton Orient. There was now a rift between the fans and Barry Fry as Mr Boizot the Chairman backed him as being on the Supporters Club with Chris Wayte this became a very worrying time for us for something we did voluntary. Spirits were lifted when we had a run of good results starting with a 2-0 win at home to Plymouth Argyle with Steve Clarke and Steve Castle scoring a loss at Darlington was followed by three wins on the bounce against Mansfield Town, Barnet and Hull City.

The 2-1 defeat at Cheltenham could have been the day our coach got stuck in a field with dodgy navigation from dear Brenda Collison and the game meant a long time out for Mark Tyler with a shoulder injury. Not really showing play off form wins against York City at home with Jason Lee and Andy Clarke scoring in a 2-1 they were forging a good partnership Andy Clarke again netting the only goal at Shrewsbury Town then we had a run of five draws in six games but we were still in fifth place. Three game run of wins beating Exeter City, Rochdale and Halifax Town 2-1 with John Cullen a midfielder signed late in the season from Sheffield United and Andy Clarke. A crowd of over 8,000 saw us slip up to Torquay United 2-0 at home but our place was secured with a Ritchie Hanlon goal at the smelly Diva Stadium think it was built on a manure heap the home of Chester City who were going round with buckets to save the club they had finished bottom of the division and were relegated.

The Posh were one step away from a trip to Wembley again in a season of upset of the field. We had to face Barnet who finished in sixth place luckily Mark Tyler was fit to play and David Oldfield ex Leicester City was brought into the starting line up we took the lead on the sloping Underhill pitch at Barnet with Jason Lee scoring very early but Posh player in waiting Mark Arber levelling but Andy Clarke scored the winner and a lead to take back to London Road. But in the second leg Barnet were blown away in front of a crowd of over 10,500 with David Farrell scoring a famous hat trick and still got his roots at the club as Head of Coaching and often the club spy at forthcoming opponent's matches.

Now the Posh were back at Wembley and we were going from a season's average gate of just over 6,500 to taking 20,000 fans and followers alike down the A1 for another chapter in the club's history. The final was to be on a Friday night and the last of the Play Offs to be played at the old Wembley and was against Darlington who after throwing away with a terrible run in at the end of the campaign which meant a long hike for their supporters. I was in charge of the convoy of about 20 coaches that made the journey from the Supporters Club on a dreadful night when the heavens opened all day long and we were very lucky to have a match at all. For some reason Anne decided to come out of the woodwork and come to Wembley but was not so keen waiting for all coaches coming in the last one getting in 15 minutes before kickoff. Then we went to our seats and were on the front row next to the bench next to Barry Fry and Wayne Turner the latest of Barry Fry's assistants.

Top player for Darlo was the beefy centre forward Marco Gabbiadini top of the scoring charts in the division we hoped that the sodden pitch was not going to be of his liking but Mike Dean coming up the referee's ranks gave it the go ahead. Darlo and especially Gabbiadini came the closest to scoring. But with 15 minutes to go Andy Clarke had to bites at the cherry in putting the ball by keeper Andy Collette. The little fat man did his usual sprint along the touch line to honour the 18th goal of the season scored by Andy Clarke and the most important one. Posh were on top for the rest of the game but had to thank Mark Tyler's agility as well. Can still see Peter Boizot, trotting on to the pitch with Cup in hand and the top on his head but of course feeling sorry for the Darlington fans and the long trek home to the North East.

The next morning saw the team on an open topped tour of the city to the Town Hall Barry Fry had delivered success at last. Was this going to heal the differences with him and some fan groups? There was to be more drama as Barry Fry had been supposedly been sacked by the board over a row over the Youth policy but later Peter Boizot said it was a misunderstanding and he remained manager for the next season. During the close season I on another of my treks walking from Boston to Abbotsbury near Weymouth along the Macmillan Way which took me through 13 counties a journey of over 300 miles plus add ones when I got lost as being on my own with no back up the journey took two and a half weeks and I managed to raise over £8,000 for the Macmillan Fund.

**BACK TO REALITY**

Barry Fry played the same record again in season 2000/1 the club had no money how many times we had heard this before. Richard Forsyth a classy midfielder joined us and a couple went the other way. A first day win at Oxford United our last trip to Headington before they moved to Kassam Stadium next season with a lone David Farrell goal then a crowd of just under 7,000 saw a 2-2 home draw against Bristol Rovers and another away win 4-1 at Oldham Athletic with Andy Clarke, Francis Green. Peter Whittingham brought in short term on loan to replace injured Jason Lee and an own goal.

Our involvement in the Football League Cup was brief going out at home in extra time in the second leg against Luton Town. Two away loses at Stoke City and at Wigan Athletic saw us below half way in the table a position we were to remain all the season. We had also gone five games with only netting once a John Cullen winner at home to Reading. We lost to the tune of 4-1 at home to Millwall with Tony Shields scoring. We now signed Leon McKenzie permanently remembered for his spell in the late eighties at he soon got out of the blocks scoring in 3-1 home win against Colchester United along with Jason Lee and Andy Clarke. After a 1-1 draw away to Mansfield Town in Round One we had no trouble in the replay winning 4-0 which gave us a home tie against Oldham Athletic in Round Two which ended 1-1 with a Jason Lee goal at the death.

The replay at Boundary Park the second highest ground in England and certainly the coldest on the night of the replay saw us go through with a lone Richard Forsyth strike and Mark Tyler playing out of his skin. The prize a trip to Stamford Bridge, to play the mighty Chelsea. The local derby just before Christmas resulted in a 2-1 defeat by Northampton Town in front of nearly 10,000 fans 'despite a Leon McKenzie goal. Tickets for the Chelsea game were a problem the club only given 3,000 if we wanted any more we had to buy a few thousand up front and the club could not take the chance. Chelsea fielded a full side the F.A, Cup was still valued by Premier clubs not like today playing reserve sides in it. Chelsea gave us plenty of room early on before two goals before half time by Zola and further strikes from Gudjohnsen, Poyet and a cheeky back heel from Zola and the hosts won 5-0.But the club had a good pay day playing in front of a crowd of 31,000. The cup defeat was carried over to the league and we went on run of seven games including going out of the Leyland Daf trophy at home to Barnet and were slipping down the league with a small squad and not many options. We did manage to win two games on the trot both at home to Wigan Athletic 2-0 with Simon Rea and Martin Williams scoring followed by a 3-2 win against Wycombe Wanderers with Leon McKenzie netting a couple and Jason Lee. The trip to Port Vale was a disaster the Valliant's running up a 5-0 win due to illness and players injured we could not provide our five substitutes on the bench we would have been well short with today's quota.

To balance the books Adam Drury one of the jewels from our Youth system was sold to Norwich City for £500,000. Gates were holding up well despite the form and for the local derby against Cambridge United we had a gate of over ten thousand and they witnessed a 4-1 win to us with four different scorers being Richard Forsyth, Francis Green, David Farrell and Jason Lee the result meant that Posh were safe from relegation. The last eight games saw only three victories beating Bristol Rovers on the Saturday 2-1 away then Bristol City on the Tuesday at home by the same score line. Also recording a 2-0 win at home to Walsall. Last game of the season brought a bumper crowd of over 11,000 mainly to celebrate Rotherham United finishing Runners up behind Millwall. But at least we stayed up finishing 12th with an average gate of over 6,000 how Darragh McAnthony would like that this season.

**SAME OLD STORY**

Once again no money available for season 2001/2 so we delved into the free transfer market the best of the bunch being Jimmy Bullard and Tommy Williams both from West Ham United neither managed to break into the first team. Also Neil Fenn who had limited first team appearances at Tottenham Hotspur. After a goalless start at Swindon David Farrell opened our account for the second season on the trot earning us a home 1-1 draw to Cardiff City.

We knocked out Swansea City in the First Round League Cup now a one game footing with Neale Fenn and Andy Clarke netting. We had to go four league games before we recorded a win against Chesterfield away with Leon McKenzie netting the lone goal. Nearly 9,000 saw us take the county bragging rights beating Cambridge United 1-0 with a Gary McDonald goal. A day still etched in peoples mind 9/11/2001 for the terrible events that took place was also the night that we lost in the Second Round of the League Cup after penalties to Coventry City. We went goal crazy hammering Bournemouth at home 6-0 with goals from Marc Joseph, Jimmy Bullard, Leon McKenzie, Daniel French and a couple from Neale Fenn. Posh were now scoring for fun at least at London Road the next game saw a 4-1 win against Bristol City with Andy Clarke netting a couple, Marc Joseph and Jimmy Bullard and Posh now in the top ten and it was going to get better two wins away to Wrexham 2-1 and home to Northampton Town with Jimmy Bullard and Andy Clarke netting in front of 8,000 fans for the local derby next home game saw us rise to fourth with a 3-2 win over Blackpool with Leon McKenzie pair and Tom Williams after they had gone two goals up very early bet the chants of two nil up and you have fxxxxd it up was ringing round the ground now up to fourth and the natives were happy. But despite the goal spree going on at home the next game beating Q.P.R. 4-1 with Neale Fenn getting two plus goals from David Farrell and Leon McKenzie we fell to fifth. We managed to net four again in the next home game a 4-1 victory against Q.P.R. with Neale Fenn netting twice and further goals from David Farrell and Leon McKenzie.

In the next six games we only picked up a single point and a 0-0 draw in the F.A. Cup 1st Round at Bedford Town although in the replay we beat them 2-1 with goals from Andy Clarke and Neale Fenn but we went out of the L.D.T.

on golden goal at Ashton Gate to Bristol City 2-1. Next week end saw us go through to the Third Round of the F.A. Cup beating A.F.C. Bournemouth by a single goal by Helgi Danielson goal. Two more defeats and a goalless draw at Cambridge United saw us slump to 17th in the table. But two further wins sent with confidence to take on Darlington now getting ready to move to the ill fated Reynolds Stadium away from the cricket ground surroundings and the cobble streets around the Feethams ground we came from 2-0 down to force a draw with David Farrell and Jimmy Bullard netting from the spot.

We made no mistake in the replay which had a home 4th Round Tie at home to Newcastle United at stake winning 2-0 with a goal from Leon McKenzie and a late one from Andy Clarke in front of nearly 11,000 fans. Sky chose the Newcastle United game to be on Match of the Day Live and remember being in very early in the morning helping grounds man Derek getting the drenched pitch fit which was going to be a leveller no squad side from Bobby Robson. They coasted to a 2-0 interval lead but Barry Fry must have leashed a few F words at them in the break one of the Newcastle United defenders put a rocker header by Shay Given then David Farrell leveller the scores and then we were going to be heartbroken when referee Neil Barry awarded them a spot kick after ball hit Leon McKenzies arm and Alan Shearer obliged then they added another to send the visitors home in 14,000 crowd home happy. Barry Fry said afterwards a replay would have netted the club another £500,000 and his comment about the game was typical There is no better duo than Bobby Robson and Alan Shearer to win the F.A.Cup. Lucky bastards but Bazz they didn't win it they went out in Round Six to the Arsenal. League form deserted us after the cup run and the next eight games only four points collected all from draws and we were down to 17th place. Two wins out of the next three games against A.F.C. Bournemouth with youth product Matthew Gill and Leon McKenzie netting the next home game against Nott's County sticks in my mind not for the result we lost by the only goal but the fact that Ideal World where I worked was burned to the ground heard all the fire engines on route to it though I was going to be out of a job in my fifties but thankfully they looked after me well as I'd been with them from day one.

A five goal rout at home to Tranmere Rovers 5-0 lifted the fans spirits thanks to Leon McKenzie hat trick and a couple from Heilgi Danielsson. The club splashed out some of the F.A. Cup coffers by signing Tom Williams from Birmingham City for £350,000 he was to return several times over his career in the game either permanent or on loan. We looked nearly safe now only six games to go but did not make it easy for ourselves beating Wycombe Wanderers

2-1 with Leon McKenzie and Francis Green scoring and a last game win at home to Bury 2-1 with Leon McKenzie scoring twice taking him to 18 league goals for the campaign and Posh finished in 17th place. Despite the lowly finished Mark Tyler was named in the Second Division P, F.A team

The close season of 2002/3 saw big signing Howard Forrinton released one of biggest disappointments can remember at the club. Barry Fry only brought in young full back Adam Newton from West Ham United and Roger Willis a midfielder from Southend United. The season started on a high note with a 3-2 success at Luton Town with Francis Green, Adam Newton and Andy Clarke netting they were going to be the only ones for seven games including a Football League Cup loss 2-0 at Portsmouth a total of over 700 minutes elapsed before Andy Clarke scored against Plymouth Argyle with Francis Green adding a second Posh were down in 20th place.

Andy Clarke was not flavour of the month with Brentford fans when Paul Smith was left stranded by a back pass and instead of kicking in he got down on his knees and headed the ball over the line in the last minute adding to Simon Reas early goal and others from Bradley Allen, Jimmy Bullard and David Farrell in a 5-1 victory. The next seven t games saw us only pick up a meagre two points with draws at Nott's County and Mansfield Town. Shades of the Checkertrade Trophy, as we went out of Leyland D.A.F Trophy at Leyton Orient 3-2 with under a thousand present. F.A. Cup involvement fell at the first fence not even got a name in the Grand National losing 3-2 at Rochdale despite the delicious fish and chips in Willbuts Lane and Neale Fenn and Andy Clarke netting. Next game was a 3-1 home defeat against Barnsley and now down bottom but one the next eight games passed and only one win in early December home to Cheltenham Town 4-1 the first time apart from the Rochdale result we had scored more than a single goal we went crazy with Jason Lee and Andy Clark scoring a couple each. We were handicapped when Mark Tyler was injured but we had a very capable replacement Lee Harrison joining from Barnet with over 200 games for them his spell was going to last twelve games but he came a fans favourite, manager Barry Fry was not so popular.

Perhaps the best result in our winless run was the 0-0 draw at home to the Cobblers in front of the biggest gate of the season well over 7,000 but at the end of the campaign they were relegated and if things did not improve we would join them. but still have the memories of 1-1 draw at Colchester United's old Layer Road ground where me and Edwin Overland had to scale a vertical ladder and walk across to the press box or crow's nest after beating Huddersfield with Andy Edwards netting the lone goal and defeat at Port Vale we beat the

Cobblers at Sixfields with Andy Clarke scoring and we were up to seventeenth. That game was going to send us on a decent run with including this game on five match unbeaten run with three draws and wins at Stockport County 2-0 with Andrew Fortiadis and Mark Arber who still lives in the area scouting this region for Manchester City netting and next game with Leon McKenzie welcome back after a long period out injury scoring a Fergie time lone goal at Crewe Alexandra.

What a journey next game on the trek we all away supporters hate and we perhaps could have it coming up again in the near future to Plymouth Argyle and got a trashing 6-1 not helped by us netting two for them now doing summarising on Radio Cambridgeshire with Edwin Overland mostly for away games how do you defend a defeat up like that only too say we were cxxx. The result putting us down to 18th place think the game at Wycombe Wanderers was when a little fat man no not the manager this one has a bald head tried to be ball boy climbing over the fence to throw no pelt the ball at the keeper urging him not to waste time to no avail we lost 2-1 Adi did you see the end of the game. We had bonanza of goals at Mansfield Town with Leon McKenzie, Simon Rea, Andy Clarke, Andrew Fotiadis and classy full back Ian Hendon signed on loan from Tottenham Hotspurs. Three wins on the bounce assured our survival at Barnsley not still a very good hunting ground for us this being a welcome exception Mark Arber and help hand with own goal in 2-1 win followed by two home games against and success against Cardiff City and Blackpool. Andy Clarke was not on the Brentford fans Christmas card list after his comical goal earlier in the season as the season fizzled out with us finishing in 11th place. Goals scored were very disappointing only netting 51 times and scoring more at away games we certainly missed Leon McKenzie when he was out with injury for a long while.

**GOULDEN TIMES AGAIN?**

The 2003/4 season opened with Barry Fry still in charge not to liking of some fans. In close season not many signings one of note was Andy Legg the Welsh international Callum Willock from Fulham and Curtis Woodhouse from Birmingham City but despite we only managed two wins in the first six games a 3-0 win home to Brentford and a lone goal scored by Andy Clarke at Notts County then we went on a horrendous run no victory in 13 games we were in 21st position but we did beat Torquay United 3-2 in the L.D.T. First Round with Dave Farrell, scoring the winning silver goal.

Things did improve but not in the division as we hoped as we reached the Third Round of the L.D.V. beating Brentford 3-2 with Leon McKenzie netting a pair and Richard Logan he also was on target next game in the First Round of the F.A. Cup at home to Hereford United with Callum Willock scoring as well. November was a good month apart from the two cup results we also had wins away at Bournemouth with Leon McKenzie and Curtis Woodhouse strikes and then another away win at Wycombe by the same margin with Leon McKenzie and Richard Logan scoring but still in the bottom four. Grimsby Town were our visitors in Round Two of the F.A. Cup Posh triumphed 3-2 Andy Clarke, Steve Thomson a recent signing from Crystal Palace and Adam Newton two losses followed against Northampton in the L.D.V. and Wrexham.

The Rushden and Diamonds game was the Posh's 2,000th game in the Football League and before the game Max Griggs their Chairman presented us with a Salver which is somewhere in the archives at the club certainly not in the Boardroom cabinet we were not very respectful beating them in our first home win a week before Christmas with Callum Willock, Curtis Woodhouse and David Farrell in a 3-1 win. We went out of the F.A. Cup in Round Three at Coventry City 2-1 with Andy Clarke netting. Then we went goal crazy putting five past Notts. County Richard Logan netting a couple in front of a poor crowd under 4,000 they were relegated at the end of the campaign. Enter Bobby Gould to help a struggling Barry Fry out he brought in hard man centre half Guy Branston from Rotherham United at first things did not go to plan as we went on an a eight game run with only three draws against Brentford, Stockport County, and a lively visit to Q.P.R. where they were trying to get the owners out and become a bit unsavoury and we only netted four times.

Had to wait from the start of January to the start of March to record another win against Barnsley 1-0 on a bitter Yorkshire night at the drab Oakwell thanks to a Callum Willock goal. Next game the short trip to Rushden and Diamonds talked then Supporters Club Chairman Andy Jardine in walking the 28 odd miles to Irthlingborough a short trip for me a seasoned walker but like John O, Grouts to Lands End to him but he managed it before kickoff time and we raised about £2,000 for the Rudolf Appeal to send sick and disabled children to Disney Land Paris and I had the pleasure of going with them on one of their holidays sadly no longer running after many years of hard work from John and Judy Fox and a very hard working committee a sad loss to the city never in my opinion got the praise they deserved. We were joined for the presentation of the cheque by David Seaman think when he came to be inducted into the Posh Hall of Fame. The journey was fruitful as well we won by a lone Callum Willock strike Andy was not keen on walking home that was not the plan so we came home on the Supporters Clubs coach.

Next game Wrexham were knocked for six revenge for the seventies result Callum Willock netting twice, Clive Platt, Sagi Burton, Andy Clarke and David Farrell handing out a 6-1 victory. Goals scored were now a premium not scoring in the next three games a 4-1 win at home saw us move out of the bottom up to 20th position a good result as visitors Swindon Town were in the promotion bracket Adam Newton, David Farrell, Richard Logan and Steve Thomson doing the damage. A draw at Oldham Athletic and a 3-1 win at Port Vale where they charged £25 to park the coach and it's still the same today went and had a word with their secretary but we did not get a discount but we got the points and they missed out on the play offs so sad for them.

We thought we were safe as a nice gap had appeared but two defeats against Brighton and Hove Albion and Bournemouth put us back in the mix. The last game of the season at Blackpool made us practically safe winning 4-1 with Curtis Woodhouse netting twice, Callum Willock and David Farrell the season ended with a home draw against bottom club Wycombe Wanderers and with Rushden and Diamonds losing and being relegated this could have been the start of the clubs demise to eventually folding and the ground now demolished. The season had improved after Bobby Gould had arrived having a of nearly fifty per cent success after joining fans favourite was certainly not Barry Fry again was Bobby Gould going to take over the reins next term.

## BACK IN THE BASEMENT AGAIN.

Bobby Gould was appointed Barry Fry's right hand man given a two year contract we opened 2004/5 season with a home win against Tranmere Rovers Sagi Burton scoring the lone goal but his time in the job was going be very brief we were not to win again until game four after draw away at Bradford City and a loss also away at Colchester United then managing to beat Brentford 3-0 at home with Clive Platt, Andy Legg and Andy Clarke scoring. League Cup did not go beyond First Round going out to M.K. Dons at the green garbed Hockey Stadium 2-0 again we could not find the net games against Huddersfield Town, Blackpool and Bristol City only scoring once in a one all draw against the Terriers through Curtis Woodhouse.

A win at Swindon with the only goal scored by full back Steve Jenkins signed from Nott's County after a long career at Huddersfield Town. Two further loses to Hull City 3-2 at home and away 2-1 to Luton Town now we were down to

19th place and London Road was not a happy place and it was to get worse in the next game in the L.D.T. at Bristol City the teams went in at half time with Posh trailing 1-0 I was on the air with Edwin Overland and noticed after the break it was only Barry Fry and Gordon the kit man on the bench but no Bobby Gould we pointed it out on air and we found later we had a scoop he had resigned had a phone call from the Sports Editor in the morning thanking me for my observance and we were once again looking for a number two Posh went out 1-0. It was another before another maximum a 3-0 with Peter Kennedy, Callum Willock and Andy Legg netting the fans was showing their displeasure with the gate being under 4,000 with the club now down to 19th the F.A. Cup 1st Round gave us some respite beating Tranmere Rovers with Peter Kennedy and a late Curtis Woodhouse seeing us through 2-0.

Wayne Purser a free transfer from troubled Hornchurch scored in his debut at Walsall in a 2-1 defeat and was on target again in a warm up for the Cup game along with David Farrell, Andre Bouchard and Curtis Woodhouse winning 4-0 at home to Port Vale. Callum Willock scored both goals as we breezed by non league Bath City 2-0. No let up in the league form even the appointment of Jimmy Quinn could help the slide and the next seven games only brought ht two draws away 1-1 at M.K. Dons with Leon Consterdines only club for the club cost us nothing at all later went to Torquay United for 75 pence no sorry £75,000.and a 2-2 draw at home to Luton Town who finished as champions. The fans had to wait to the 3rd of the F.A. for a favourable result beating M.K. Dons 2-0 with Richard Logan and returning Mark Arber netting another three games with draws against Wrexham and Hull City and a loss to Oldham Athletic we were down to 23rd position and we were losing touch of the teams just above us. A big following went to the 4th Round of the F.A. Cup away to Nottingham Forest we lost 1-0 to a Marlon King strike they were relegated at the end of the campaign.

The win against Stockport who was bottom was nothing to get excited about again less than 4,000 fans bothering to attend the glory fans had gone back into the woodwork as the Cup run ended Callum Willock and Richard Logan on target in 2-1 win. Then over a hundred of us went on the long trip to Torquay United and it was an even longer journey home after losing 2-1 was it worth it we all asked ourselves.

Got back on track after another two defeats against Doncaster Rovers and Sheffield Wednesday at Chesterfield winning 3-1 with Wayne Purser netting a couple and Richard Logan. Another long journey took us to Tranmere Rovers on a Friday evening they were going well and handed us a 5-0 hiding with yours truly on the air you have to choose your words could not say we were crap the best thing of the evening was the pretty policewomen who came on the bus to welcome us. Before the 3-0 home defeat against Colchester United the news was announced which pleased many fans that Barry Fry was resigning as manager saying that the fans have had enough of me after nine seasons he would remain as owner but thinks hopefully it's for the best things will change next season.

The Colchester United result started another run of five games without a victory we went to Blackpool and gave us welcome win 1-0 win Callum Willock scoring but 2-0 reverse at Walsall our fate was sealed as we had to get three wins out of three and score a lot of goals and we only registered 47 for the whole season. Kick in the teeth was that our popular rivals M.K. Dons beat us 3-0 at home to help them to avoid relegation. With losing the last game at Port Vale we finished 23rd twelve points from M.K. Dons who were lucky to survive as Wrexham became the first side to be docked ten points for going into administration but that was no consolation to us and our return to the bottom tier once again.

**WRIGHT OR RON**

After sifting through all the numerous applications Barry Fry reported that the new manager for the new season 2005/6 was to be ex England player Mark Wright he should have all the credentials as a player with his 45 caps but his management career had been a bit chequered and had drawn the wrath of the F.A. As his number two he brought Steve Bleasdale his assistant at his previous club Chester City and a well respected coach. He pleased the fans with his signings bringing in eight new ones and letting ten go including the popular Andy Clarke and Andy Legge and selling Curtis Woodhouse to Hull City at a bargain price of £25,000 he was later to turn Professional Boxer and became British Light Welterweight Champion for five months and had a career record of 22 wins in 29 fights.

Lots of money was made when Manchester United honoured Barry Fry with visiting London Road in his testimonial game as he was a budding youngster with them until injury put paid to his career. All the stars turned out at we were beaten 6-0. The first game was against believe it or not against the managements old team Chester City at home and they recorded a lone goal victory then followed by the same score line at Carlisle United. First win came at Bristol Rovers a 3-2 victory due to a coach problem missed the first goal and was on air when Adam Newton netted and only just got settled when David Farrell netted another Richard Logan netting a third in a 3-2 victory followed by 2-0 win at home to Mansfield Town with David Farrell and Shaun St Ledger on target.

No league cup progress as we went out first game at Plymouth Argyles Home Park no we were 300 miles from home losing 2-1 with Chris Plummer netting. Two draws and a 2-0 away win at neighbours Rushden and Diamonds with Richard Logan and close season signing from Lincoln City classy midfielder Peter Gain bringing home the points and we were just inside the play off positions at early doors. Loss by the only at home to Grimsby Town was followed by a 2-1 win at Lincoln City with James Quinn netting a poor excuse for our former player by the same surname Jimmy and Adam Newton scoring then we went a run of no points from three games but our first visit to Macclesfield was fruitful winning 4-0 with Dave Farrell netting twice, Danny Crow and Callum Willock. On the air at Cheltenham which be fair the floodlights were rubbish both me and Edwin both got the Posh scorer wrong in the 2-1 defeat and was reminded by Tommy Robson at Boston who was on air for the local derby another loss 1-0 at least we will get the scorer right today he shouted across the road. Just under 1,500 bothered attending and had to endure extra time when Posh put Bristol Rovers out of the L.D.T. 2-1. We ourselves had the indignity of being put out of the 1st Round by then non league club Burton Albion after a goalless draw at London Road the replay at the Pirelli Stadium on Sea the pitch had as much sand on it as Hunstanton beach and that was in November we lost 1-0 and never came to terms with the pitch the same as Manchester United in the Third Round taking them back to Old Trafford.

We had a crisis on the broadcast as Edwin's transmitter batteries were dead and had to go to the local corner shop to get some and then after the crisis on the pitch we had to send a search party out for dear old Duncan who had lost his bearings. At the week end the long journey to Wrexham saw a 1-1 draw with Danny Crow scoring with I think Darren Ferguson in midfield for the Dragons less than a thousand fans turned up for the 2-1 win in the 2nd Round L.DV Trophy against Swindon Town. Ryan Semple now coach for our U18 side scored in an unhappy return to Mark Wright former team Chester City going down 3-1 and then netted again along with Callum Willock to end a five game winless run beating Nott's County at home 2-0. Despite this we were still in the top half of the league.

Fewer than fifty fans made the long journey to Swansea City and it was the end of our run in L.D.V. trophy losing 3-1 and made it an even longer night as went into extra time. We saw the year out with three away matches on the bounce drawing against Mansfield Town in goalless game before a win against

Northampton Town with a single goal of the game scored by Chris Plummer in nearly a full house at Sixfields. Things were on the up for the club or so it seemed with two more wins in a week in early January with home wins 4-1 against Bury and Rushden and Diamonds with hard tackling Dean Holden and James Quinn netting in a 2-0 victory and another home goalless draw to Oxford United pushed us into a playoff position but very surprisingly Barry Fry put all the players up for sale first one out of the door was Sagi Burton after nearly a hundred games for the club to Shrewsbury Town. At the end of January the hot seat at London Road was empty again with Mark Wright surviving only 35 games it was a strange sacking as the team was in such a good position but the reason was given as breach of club discipline. The club then appointed his assistant Steve Bleasedale his number two as caretaker boss his only management experience was as manager of Leigh R.M.I. in non league. His first game resulted in a win at Grimsby Town 2-1 with Peter Gain and Danny Crow netting this was tainted with the news that Callum Willock was going to Brentford for £50,000 had a good ratio of goals in games played but suffered with long spells out with injuries. Two wins on the trot for the new boss Richard Logan netting the only goal in the home defeat of Cheltenham Town. His first setback was defeat at Shrewsbury Town 2-1 but bounced back with Mark Arber netting both goals in 2-1 defeat at home to Darlington. The club were now going to have a £100,000 windfall not from the sale of a player but from Sky Ron Atkinson ex Manchester United manager who was to join the club as a trouble-shooter for the rest of the season the results were to be shown on a programme called Big Ron Manager why the club thought it was necessary as Steve Bleasdale had lead us to sixth in the table with 15 points out of a possible 21. Things became fraught between Bleasdale and Atkinson mainly due to the attitude of young players Danny Crow and Sean St. Ledger who did themselves no good for their attitude towards Bleasdale on the air.

The money was talking from Sky but not doing the club or its image any good. Had dealings with Ron Atkinson as shared on air summarising the game away to one of his old clubs Oxford United I did the first half with my few notes and he did the second half with his charts which covered all the table did no good as were awful and lost to the only goal of the game. The loss by the odd goal at home to Northampton Town made things worse and the pair were always at loggerheads regards players, tactics etc. Play offs were still on the cards with a 3-1 win away at Bury with Danny Crow scoring twice and Adam Newton and in 7th place. The next two games brought thinks to a head both defeats at home to Boston United and away to Rochdale by the only goal of both games. It seemed that Steve Bleasdale wanted to drop Sean St. Ledger for the Macclesfield game but Barry Fry went against him as scouts were looking at him and he picked the side with this Steve Bleasdale resigned in front of the cameras a sad day for the image of the club but it proved later to be a god send for the future. After all the trouble the team beat Macclesfield 3-2 with Danny Crow netting twice and David Farrell his last goal for the club. We needed to win both our remaining games to get in the Play offs but lost both away to Leyton Orient and home to Wycombe Wanderers. Posh finished the season in 9th place nine points off a play off place. The next season was going to see the arrival of our savour and for me to me and my wife Anne going to bring us heartbreak as a family.

**THE MONEY MAN ARRIVES**

One good thing that arrived out of the Big Ron programme was in early season Darragh McAnthony joined after taking perhaps pity on the club how it portrayed the club on the television and wanted to buy the club from Barry Fry this pleased certain groups that they thought Fry would be leaving this was not be and he is still part of the furniture today in spirit but not in body as he says nothing works properly now turned seventy two years old. The start of the season 2006/7 saw the appointment of Keith Alexander as manager joining from Lincoln City played under Barry Fry at Barnet and managed locally at Stamford and other top non league teams in the area. Perhaps not a popular choice but fans had to remember we were living on Barry's Frys money and his efforts to keep the club afloat. Sean St. Ledger brought welcome funds being transferred to Preston North End for £225,000 a good deal as he had come through our Youth ranks one not popular decision was the end of David Farrell's career at least as a player at London Road after nine years at the club and 388 appearances scoring 52 times always seemed to be one of Barry Frys most popular substitutions think number seven was his least favourite number he moved to Boston United.

Some of the transfer money was spent on bringing in Ben Futcher from Grimsby Town and Guy Branston rejoined the club. The season got a flying start a 4-1 win at home to Bristol Rovers 4-1 with goals from Jamie Day, Richard Butcher, Simon Yeo and Lloyd Opara his only goal for the club and then Simon Yeo scoring in the victory at Boston United then a goalless draw at Wrexham and a 3-1 win at home to Macclesfield with Trevor Benjamin scoring a pair and a own goal and we were in 2nd place. Ipswich Town provided the visitors for the First Round of the League Cup going into extra time 2-2 at the end of that with goals from Trevor Benjamin and Guy Branston but we went through on spot kicks. Our good form eluded us just before the new owner took over with four defeats on the trot including a 5-0 defeat at Walsall but we got back on track with a 1-0 win away to a Swindon Town side going well with a lone Trevor Benjamin strike.

Darragh McAnthony joined the club on the eve of our League Cup Second Round game at home to Everton the only time the teams have meet the crowd was just under 11,000 buoyed by a new owner and a Cup upset this was not to be going down to a late goal 2-1 with Trevor Benjamin again netting we suffered a hangover from that game going down 5-3 at London Road to Hartlepool's United with goals from Peter Gain, Richard Butcher and hard tackling Dean Holden not a good welcome for the new owner. A draw at home to Barnet with a lone Peter Gain goal saw a run of three wins with wins against Stockport County and Milton Keynes away and a 2-1 win at home to Shrewsbury with Trevor Benjamin and Danny Crow scoring and a draw 2-2 at home to Grimsby Town saw us up to 7th place. Rotherham were our opponents in the F.A. Cup First Round winning 3-0 at home with new loan signing from non league side Greys Athletic Aaron McLean scoring his first goal on a great career at the club along with Danny Crow and Richard Butcher in a 3-0 victory he also netted he also was on target the next two games victories 2-0 away to Mansfield Town and a 5-2 win at home to Torquay United with Shane Huke, Ben Futcher, Richard Butcher and a helping from a visitor.

Johnstones Paint Trophy now replacing the L.D.V. Saw Posh go out by the only goal in the long haul to Bristol Rovers, but at the week end putting out Tranmere Rovers in the Second Round of the F.A. Cup at home 2-1 with Danny Crow scoring a brace. One more win followed at Rochdale with a lone Aaron McLean netting saw the team go in free fall going ten league games without a win and going out of the F.A. Cup after a draw at London Road and losing the replay at Home Park in these games we only scored seven goals and slipped into the bottom half of the table. Only good things to happen on the terrible run was the signings of George Boyd from Stevenage for £260,000 and the loans of Aaron McLean now a prolific scorer for club and Craig Morgan from Milton Keynes were made permanent. During the run manager Keith Alexander left the club by mutual consent being replaced by one of my favourite players in the lower divisions Darren Ferguson midfield general from Wrexham along with his number two Kevin Russell a popular loan signing in the early nineties at the club. His first two games at home to Swindon Town resulted in a 1-1 draw with Peter Gain scoring and then a 3-2 loss at Bristol Rovers with Danny Crow and Aaron McLean netting. I was very upset by this game after being used a summariser alongside Edwin Overland on Radio Cambridgeshire at most away games especially the long hauls was replaced by my old mate Bob Burrows not his fault bless him and never been used again perhaps I was cxxx at it this was something I really enjoyed.

The new manager's first win came against his old club Wrexham at London Road with Aaron McLean, George Boyd, and a Wrexham player who he had offered a fiver to put one in his own net. On a personal nature thinks were not good Sharon Anne had left her husband along with her son our grandson Harry who they had adopted and was now living with us and we had to spend time with them especially as he had A.D.H.D. and was a handful so my away trips were put on hold. Craig Mackail-Smith arrived from Dagenham under a cloud of controversy between the two clubs for £125,000 and also Shane Blackett for £100,000 from the same club who to me was a terrible disappointment and Gavin Strachan who in later years like he is at Doncaster Rovers has been Fergies number two. The 3-0 win away to Bury with MacKail Smith scoring the his first for the club along with Ben Futcher and Gavin Strachan the next two games both wins 2-0 to Nott's County and 4-0 to M.K.D saw us back in the top ten which was our finishing position. The rest of the season became a blur as on the 28th March the day she should have signed for a property for her and Harry Sharon Anne had a series of three strokes which took her right side she could not walk or use her arm and it also made her blind we were told to prepare for the worst the worse day of our lives so far for us as a family football was of no importance any more perhaps being selfish said how can that man up their treat Sharon Anne and us this way for all the good work I have done for charity and backing me this was not fair play.

## COMING TO TERMS WITH LIFE

Sharon Anne was in hospital for ten weeks in the Stroke Ward and because we were nearly living at the hospital Harry was looked after by his father who brought him to see her at weekends. When she was discharged from hospital she came to us on a hospital bed living in our dining room. My involvement with the club ceased as only on home Saturdays that she was having good days and we did not have Harry did I manage to get to the games gave up my roles of ground tours, Forever Posh Committee and working on the pitch. Missed perhaps the best years in modern days of the club but as time moved on Sharon Anne and Anne encouraged me to go to matches and used to go to the nearer away games and especially when Sharon Anne made the heartbreaking decision not to have Harry visit any more after her now ex husband had his hands on me and the police wanted me to press charges which I did not.

If I did not go away I visited local games at Stamford now hard to get to as moved ground, Yaxley or Northern Star and took my radio to listen to the Posh game. Will not go into the season from then to now in depth as the younger fans that will hopefully know what has happened in the years they have been coming. What did these seasons bring 2007/8 brought us promotion finishing second to M.K.D. with the Holy Trinity as Barry Fry called them Aaron McLean, Craig Mackail-Smith and George Boyd netting over fifty times between them gates up to 6,000 lots of games over a thousand travelling away but unfortunately not me many times. Run in the F.A Cup going out 3-0 at home to W.B.A. after a replay and now back in Division One. Most disappointing thing for me was that Darren Ferguson replaced my Posh Idol Mark Tyler who he never gave a chance to with Joe Lewis a nice bloke now performing well at Aberdeen.

Darragh McAnthony the money man as Sharon Anne called him as she could not get his name out after the strokes was splashing out his money at the start of the 2008/9 campaign the bargain being Russell Martin signed from Wycombe Wanderers for a giveaway price of £50,000 sorry to see Adam Newton leave the club after a poor start by the end of the year we were in the promotion bracket and stayed there all season finishing second to neighbours Leicester City a game at home that brought in over 14,000 fans and helped the gates to a seasons average of over 7,600 the Holy Trinity had performed well again MacKail Smith netting 23 times, Arron McLean 18 and playmaker George Boyd 9.

Close season 2009/10 not that I had any real interest brought Tommy Rowe to the club from Stockport County what a player he was to be at the club costing us £150,000 and the classy midfield player Lee Frecklington was signed permanently from Lincoln City for £200,000 but Mark Tyler was shown the door after 485 appearances for the Posh being second to Tommy Robson in total appearances. First game back was the same opponents as last time Derby County this time away we finished up losing 2-1. It was going to be a long season from the start with us never really moving away from the bottom four had a bit of a run in the Football League Cup getting to the Fourth Round beating Ipswich Town and then Newcastle United at home in Round Three before finally going out to Blackburn Rovers 5-2 away in the next round.

Soon Darren Ferguson was to depart as the team were rock bottom he was still popular with many fans despite the plight of the team. Mark Cooper was now in the hot seat he had to wait six games for his first maximum beating Watford 2-1 at home with us ground staff clearing the snow off when the players came out of the tunnel the goals coming from Lee Frecklington and him of a big throw and nothing else Exodus Geohaghon netting. Due to my working pattern had to work Bank Holidays and missed the great comeback against Cardiff City as we came back from a half time break 4-0 down but two goals from Josh Simpson, Charlie Lee and a last gasp George Boyd strike resulted in a 4-4 draw not very nice me going home from work all talking about the performance.

Mark Coopers reign did not last long being sacked with a dire record of 13 games played one victory and picking up only seven points out of a possible thirty nine and the team bottom of the division off the a massive eleven points adrift his replacement was the ex Motherwell and Stockport County manager Jim Gannon who actually played for them when we beat them at Wembley. Also he could not change results and the club had lost Paul Coutts for a much needed £700.000 to Preston North End Darren Fergusons new club the only thing he did achieve was two wins together at home to Sheffield United winning by lone Craig Mackail-Smith goal and a loan Liam Dickinson strike at Watford Posh were finally demoted back to the First Division against Barnsley in a 2-2 draw with four games still to play and Jim Gannon's short term contract came to an end. Next in revolving door was former Cambridge United manager Gary Johnson the fourth of the campaign despite the terrible season gates had held up well mainly because of the away support with Newcastle bringing over 4,000 and local rivals Leicester City bringing over 3,000 and for the last game Blackpool brought half of their present day gate nearly 2,000. Thankfully for me but not in the circumstances with Sharon Anne's condition only had to endure the home games and Edwin's docile tones on Radio Cambridgeshire.

The close season 2010/11 started with speculation that our prize assets of the Holy Trinity would be split up but revolving doors was not for once managers it was players with fifteen players moved out the pick where the transfers of Shaun Batt to Millwall for £300,000 and Welsh International centre half again to Preston North End and many other bit part players for various fees and a huge reduction in wages thus keeping our prize assets at London Road much to the pleasure of the fans and Sharon Anne now in her own flat with full time carer five minutes away as she wanted her independence. Players coming in included Lee Tomblin for £180,00 from Rushden and Diamonds a midfielder called Grant McCann from Scunthorpe United Gary Johnson was still in charge and we rattled in nineteen goals in our first six games including League Cup wins against Bristol Rovers and Cardiff City both at home the only defeat being a big one 5-1 at Bournemouth and we were sitting in promotion positions and the 5-4 defeat of Swindon Town Posh going two goals up very early at half time it was 3-3 and finally Posh won it in Fergie time sorry he had not arrived yet with the goals coming from Craig Mackail-Smith twice, Lee Frecklington, George Boyd and an own goal and we were up to second. But things were to change in the next few games we were scoring plenty of goals after half a season we had scored 48 goals but conceded 47 worse to come was that part of The Holy Trinity Aaron McLean was being transferred to Hull City a highly popular player with the fans always played with a smile on his face his fee of £1,300,000 being a big windfall for the club in his 178 starts he netted 84 times.

We reached the Third Round of the F.A. Cup with wins against Stockport County and Bury but the Third Round at Fulham was the swan song for manager Gary Johnson we lost 6-2 at Craven Cottage. David Oldfield who is now back with us as I pen this and hope that the club take him on to assist Grant McCann had a 100 per cent record as manager his only game in charge being a 2-1 home win against Brentford. Richard Butcher who played for the club a few years earlier had died suddenly with a heart condition cardiac arrhythmia at 29 years of age his death coming less than a year after Keith Alexander who had signed him for Macclesfield had passed away suddenly at 53 after suffering a brain aneurysm in 2003 both these deaths were a sad loss to the game.

Fans were very surprised when Darren Ferguson returned to the club the chairman saying he had unfinished business and wanted to work with him a long time. What a piece of magic he was going to bring to the table but unfortunately for me my games I watched were all at home think because of things at home lost interest in travelling away electing to be local. It took the new manager only two games to get us up and running beating Hartlepool's United 4-0 at home with goals from Craig Mackail-Smith, Tommy Rowe, Lee Tomlinand, James Wesolowski who promised so much but soon fell off the radar. Posh were scoring for fun beating Sheffield Wednesday at home 5-3 with scoring his second goal in Fergie time to claim the point along with goals from another pair from George Boyd and impact player who had so much to offer but unfortunately not at Posh Nathaniel Mendez Laing and he did blot his career off the field as well.

A 4-4 draw with big boys Southampton was good viewing for Sky watchers they were to finish runners up at the end of the campaign with Craig Mackail-Smith, two penalties each from Lee Tomblin and Grant McCann plus Chris Whelpdale who was always plagued with injury at the club. The club then went on an eight game unbeaten run with wins at Yeovil, Tranmere Rovers, a 5-0 hammering of Oldham Athletic away, wins at home to Exeter City, away to Nott's County and a 6-0 mauling of Carlisle United you had to feel sorry for the just under 400 fans who had made the 450 mile round trip the damage being done by two early goals from Craig Mackail-Smith and Tommy Rowe to be added to by a couple of George Boyd strikes, Ryan Bennett and David Ball. The 4-1 defeat at Hillsborough of Sheffield Wednesday doing the double over them with George Boyd scoring another couple, Craig Mackail-Smith and Lee Tomblin netting and we were in third position.

We started to splutter a bit losing to rivals Milton Keynes and then dropped points with two draws before getting back on track with the 2-0 away win against old boss John Stills team Dagenham and Redbridge with David Ball netting two early strikes. Little did we know when we drew 1-1 at Huddersfield Town with a Grant McCann this game was to be repeated at the end of the season with a great outcome for the club? We held on to fourth spot win 2-1 win against Plymouth Argyle at home two successive draws both two goals each against Yeovil and Rochdale and last game we trashed Dagenham and Redbridge 5-0 in front of 7,500 at home with Nathaniel Mendes Laing who had come up with some valuable goals in the run in scoring along with Grant McCann, George Boyd, Craig Mackail-Smith and David Ball meaning that we finished fourth and in the Play Off Semi Finals we had to play fifth place Milton Keynes who we finished two points above.

Did not make the short journey to the first leg with us losing to a 3-2 score line despite goals from Craig Mackail-Smith and a spot kick from Grant McCann but we managed to turn it round in midweek with a 2-0 success with goals from the scorers in front of nearly 12,000 fans. Posh were back at Wembley again but not so as the Play off Final was to be held at the Theatre of Dreams Old Trafford as the Champions League was being played there on the previous day with Huddersfield Town being our opponents. The game was watched by over 48,000 fans with a noisy 15,000 from the city with the Terriers having printed blue T Shirts for it seemed all their fans with Believe on them glad we have got a Papillion in our Lady Pip never Believed in a Terrier. I was convinced to go to the final, In goal for them was our former keeper Ian Bennett and Posh were without Joe Lewis again after his injury in the Milton Keynes game and Paul Jones replaced him neither keeper saw much action in the first period against the run of play Grant McCann took one of his trade mark free kicks and from it little Tommy Rowe netted after 78 minutes less than two further minutes we were 2-0 up with Craig Mackail-Smith scoring in which was to be his last appearance for the club this being his 35th strike of the campaign and then Grant McCann was again a provider netting another of his free kicks the three goals in six odd minutes were too much for the Town fans and the T Shirts were dumped on the terraces and could be seen by the side of the Motorway coming out of Manchester. The return of young Fergie saw us back in the Championship after only one season away and this being the third promotion in four years under him and the stewardship of Darragh McAnthony.

Season 2011/12 saw popular players Charlie Lee and injury prone Chris Whelpdale transferred to Gillingham for £150,000 each and Craig Mackail-Smith signed for Brighton and Hove Albion after 198 appearances which have been added to since and netting 99 times for a massive club record of £2,500,000 putting him third in the clubs all time scorers behind Jim Hall and Tommy Robson. Again most of the games I saw were at home early season saw us mid table who was to see the trashing of the Tractor Boys Ipswich Town at home to the tune of 7-1 in front of the Sky cameras Lee Tomblin netting a hat trick, Paul Taylor and Grant McCann a couple each firing them all by one of my favourite keepers David Stockdale who always have a chat to when he is at London Road and met him again at the E.F,L launch at Fulham at the start of the season. We could not find the net in the next three games including a 2-0 loss to Middlesbrough in Second Round of the League Cup going down 2-0 at home.

Burnley away saw us back in winning ways 2-0 with Emile Sinclair netting both and three wins in five games with wins at Portsmouth 3-2 with Lee Frecklington scoring twice and Manchester United loanee Ryan

Tunnicliffe scoring in Fergie time along with victories at Bristol City 2-1 with Lee Tomblin and George Boyd netting and then a ding dong game again at home to Cardiff City winning 4-3 with Grant McCann netting a couple assisted by goals from George Boyd and Paul Taylor. After these results we went in freefall the next nine games only saw us pick up six points and one win against Derby County at home Paul Taylor, Grant McCann and Tommy Rowe scoring in a rare victory two wins were then produced at near neighbours Nottingham Forest 1-0 with a George Boyd goal and a home win against Coventry City with Emile Sinclair scoring. In the meantime we said goodbye to Bryan Bennett transferred to Norwich City for a new club record £3,500,000 and loaned back to us as we were short of players for a month. We were out of the F.A. Cup at our first hurdle the Third Round at Sunderland 2-0.

We went all through January without a victory and to mid February before we returned to winning ways home to Bristol City doing the double with a 3-0 victory with strikes from Lee Tomblin a pair and David Ball. Help we thought was on its way with the signing of Tyrone Barnett which we were to pay a million for at the end of the season from Crawley Town but to excuse the pun he wasn't the Million Dollar Man at London Road but he did score on his debut a last minute strike coming on level the score at bottom side Doncaster Rovers. Again our strikers drew two blanks in the defeats against Millwall and Crystal Palace both loses and we were we were getting sucked in to the reaches of the relegation zone. We settled the ship with a win against Blackpool who was on the surge into the Premiership winning 3-1 at home with Tyrone Barnett, Paul Taylor and George Boyd netting. Ipswich got revenge on us at Portman Road winning 3-2. Two loses in a week did not help our cause defeats at grim Barnsley and home to West Ham in front of 13,500 odd fans with a big contingent from them as they were in the promotion slots.

Big gates were the order for the next two home games a 1-0 victory against Leicester City with Paul Taylor scoring in front of nearly 11,000 fans and that was beaten against Nottingham Forest with us losing to the only goal of the game. The last four games of the season only brought two draws at home to Watford and away to Derby and we finished on the average for survival in the Championship 50 points which was not going to be in the next season and we finished 18th and lived to fight another day in our League of Dreams. Scoring goals had not been our problem netting 67 in the league but we let in 77 at the other end.

## HEARTBREAK AT THE PALACE

Season 2012/3 brought several new faces a new keeper Bobby Olejick was signed from Torquay United for a reported £300,000 he figured in the Division Two P.F.A. team the previous season. Michael Boswick joined from Stevenage for had previously turned down a bid of £1,000,000 for him and Laurie Wilson the performances he has turned in since then would class him at worth a million plus on his own Kane Ferdinand signed for £200,000 from Southend United who turned out only to be a squad player and Nathanial Mendes-Laing and big money signing Tyrone Barnett's loans were turned permanent. We also now had a new second in command as former player Gavin Strachan replaced Mark Robson who moved to Barnet as manager. Early season was hard going we did progress in the League Cup beating Southend United at home 4-0 but going out in the next round 3-2 at Reading but in the league we had wait till game eight to put any points on the board at all after defeats against Leicester City, Millwall, Leeds United. Birmingham City through a cruel own goal by Bobby Olejnik, Burnley, Bristol City and Wolves no easy games in this Division. We broke our duck away to Hull City who were promoted at the end of the campaign winning 3-1 at the K.C. Stadium with believe it or not a Emile Sinclair hat trick and next game away at Barnsley 2-0 with goals from George Boyd and Tyrone Barnett followed by two loses home to Nottingham Forest by lone goal and the same fate away to Watford. The next game home to Huddersfield Town at the break we were 3-0 up with a couple from George Boyd and a rare Kgosi Ntlhe strike and finished up winners 3-1 then another maximum against Derby County at home we included Saido Berahino on loan from W.B.A. netted twice and Michael Bostwick winning 3-0.

Three defeats on the trot to Sheffield Wednesday, Brighton and Hove Albion and Crystal Palace thinks were not good off the field either with Tyrone Barnett, Nathaniel Mendes Laing, Emile Sinclair and club captain Gabriel Zakuani being placed on the transfer list for a breach of club discipline Barnett and Sinclair soon disappeared off the scene. Barry Fry was to find another young gem this time from Dagenham and Redbridge with the signing of striker Dwight Gayle for a reported £500,000 signed firstly on loan he opened his account scoring the only goal in a 4-1 defeat at home to Blackpool two more defeats followed 3-2 at home to Middlesbrough with Dwight Gayle scoring both and then adding to his tally along with Michael Bostwick in the 2-1 away win at Cardiff City. We went into a 3-1 lead with goals from Lee Tomblin, Dwight Gayle and the classy midfield loan player from W.B.A George Thorne before referee Nigel Miller the oldest and the fittest one outside the Premiership but never does the Posh many favours awarded a second penalty which was despatched by the visitors Gabriel Zakuani and Mark Little added further but despite a late fight back we held on to win 5-4.

Posh were now placed half way in the division in 12th place. Boxing Day for once was a happy day as we were 3-0 victor's at Wolves with Lee Tomblin, Tommy Rowe and Dwight Gayle on target. Next game away to Bristol City Lee Tomblin being shown the red card very early in the match and we went down despite goals from Grant McCanns penalty and Dwight Gayle going down 4-2. New Years day and we were up and running in 2013 with a 2-1 win to home to Barnsley with Michael Bostwick and Tommy Rowe strikes. No F.A. Cup glory as we were well beaten at the first hurdle by Norwich City 3-0 at home in front of over 13,000 fans. The short journey to Nottingham Forest resulted in a 2-1 defeat our goal being scored by Scott Wootton on loan from Darren Fergusons father at Manchester United. After two draws against Hull City and Burnley both at home we had two great results 2-1 at Leicester City the best performance of the season was the 5-1 rout of Millwall at the New Den with Lee Tomblin scoring a pair added to by Tommy Rowe, Nathaniel Mendes- Laing and George Boyd the Lions being reduced to ten men with twenty minutes to go. We had to wait another three games after defeats to Birmingham City and Bolton Wanderers before we went on a ten match unbeaten run with wins at Blackburn Rovers with Dwight Gayle netting a hat trick in a 3-2 win and won by the only goal of the game at Blackpool with Kane Ferdinand scoring followed by a 2-1 win at home to Cardiff City who finished the season as champions with two penalties in seven minutes converted by Grant McCann and a 3-2 win at Watford with Danny Swanson, Dwight Gayle and Lee Tomblin netting.

Draws with Charlton Athletic, Ipswich Town, Leeds United, Middlesbrough and Huddersfield Town and Brighton and Hove Albion took us into 20th place out of the relegation zone and over average survival points total of 50 now on 51. Derby County who had nothing to play for dimmed our hopes next game beating us 3-1 and we were back in the mire. The win against Sheffield Wednesday in our last home game 1-0 with a lone Grant McCann strike in front of a near 14,000 gate and we were now on 54 points but it became obvious this will not be enough this season and we went into the last game at Crystal Palace only needing to avoid defeat to overhaul Barnsley but Selhurst Place was to become Heartbreak Palace with Lee Tomblin putting Posh ahead before Glen Murray levelled the score we then went ahead with Nathanial Mendes-Laing putting us ahead before Kevin Phillips levelled it up with seven minutes to go and they broke our supporters hearts and mine think I was watching either Northern Star or Yaxley at the time with a dubious free kick by Dwight Gayle according to referee Craig Pawson which Mile Jedinak netted in the 89 minute which sent the club down and put our opponents into the play offs and then into the Premiership. Relegation was reported as a loss to the club of in the region of £5,000,000 the main failing of the season was our poor home form with losing 10 games and 35 points.

**A PIECE OF SILVERWARE**

Season 2013/4 is the last season that I am going to into any depth as even the little junior teams that I take round the ground remark about the celebration print that I have in my room at Wembley at the end of the season they were at the game so don't think need to remind fans however young they are. Now back watching the lads home and away not because that Sharon Anne was any better or thing s were any better with her carers with the fifty she must have had before she did you can count the good ones on one hand it was a mine field and my wife Anne was always filling in but at least my mind was at rest when she was looking after her we wished she had not moved to her flat. Darren Ferguson despite relegation was still at the helm and made a big money signing Britt Assombalonga from Watford for an undisclosed fee thought be over £1,000,000 and given a four year contract and another big signing Jack Payne a midfielder from Gillingham for £750,000 and Dwight Gayle joined Crystal Palace £6,000,000 his career at the club was brief scoring 13 times in 29 league games and was only signed for a initial £500,000 and finally George Boyd went to Hull City after an abortive move to Nottingham Forest due to a problem with his eyes according to them.

Back in Division One we were very quick off the blocks opening day win against Swindon Town with Britt Assomalonga netting the only goal followed by a 4-2 win at Nott's County and was again on target along with Tommy Rowe, Tyrone Barnett and Grant McCann then another win 2-1 at home to Oldham Athletic with again Britt Assombalonga on target with Lee Tomblin. It seemed a quick long journey home from Tranmere as we hammered them 5-0 going three up by the break through Tommy Rowe, Tyrone Barnett and a Grant McCann spot kick added to by Britt Assombalongo and Mark Little. By now we had progressed in the League Cup beating Colchester United away 5-1 and then trashing Championship side Reading 6-0 their worst defeat for 14 years with a great display of attacking football a Lee Tomblin hat trick including two penalties and further goals from Danny Swanson, Jack Payne and Britt Assombalongo put us in Round 3 to be elimininated by Sunderland at The Stadium of Light 2-0.

First defeat in the division came at home to Crawley Town despite the visitors playing for an hour with ten men. The next two games saw Tyrone Barnett scoring in each along with Michael Bostwick in a 2-2 draw and in the 3-0 win at Bristol City along with a pair from Britt Assombalonga Barnett despite being to me a flop at the club his actual record in the League shows he has netted every four games and always finds a club. The home game against Milton Keynes saw Nathaniel Knight-Percival get an early bath within the first ten minutes but then a Lee Tomblin us in front added to by a Britt Assombalonga just after the half hour the Dons pulled one back before Mark Little was shown red by referee Darren Drysdale but the nine men held on for the three points and spoiled Carl Robinsons week-end. The chant we only need nine men echoed around London Road. This win was to send us on a five match unbeaten run Grant McCann penalty netting the only goal to beat Rotherham and again on target in the 2-0 win at home to Preston North End with Tyrone Barnett adding the other and then scoring the only goal at the most expensive place to park a coach I am sure in the whole of the Football League Port Vale one of my least favourite grounds.

A win at home to Shrewsbury Town again by the only strike of the game by Nathaniel Mendes-Laing then a goalless draw at home to Sheffield United and we had beaten Brentford on our what was going to be our first step to Wembley again winning 2-1 in the Johnstones Paint Trophy. The next five games were all going to draw blanks loses against Colchester United by a lone goad with Lee Tomblin being sent off just before the hour and think that was the game where he kicked the water bottle on the motorway in temper home to Leyton Orient 3-1 with Tommy Rowe netting and a 2-0 loss at Walsall with Shaun Brisley being red carded late in the game Stevenage suffered the same fate but still managed to beat us by the only goal at home and things did not get any better losing 3-2 at Brentford with Jack Payne and Britt Assombalonga netting beaten by a late goal and a helping hand from Gabriel Zakuani.

We managed to get through the First Round of the F.A. Cup beating Exeter City 2-0 with Britt Assombalonga and Nathaniel Mendes – Laing putting us into Round Two. We ended a five game barren run securing our first ever home league win against Wolverhampton Wanderers with a Michael Bostwick goal and then we trashed Tranmere Rovers in the next round of the F.A. Cup with a Britt Assombalonga hat trick and a pair from Shaun Jeffers. Next game away to the unwelcoming ground of Gillingham after a long hike from where they park the coaches you are treated to sitting in a permanent temporary stand open to the elements we managed to get a late 2-2 draw with a Britt Assombalonga back heel adding to his earlier strike. Another ground that is in the same bracket is Newport County's Rodney Parade which primarily is a Rugby ground and it shows by the state off the pitch and the facilities as Dan our kit man had a wait while the dressing room was cleared after a Rugby training session but saying all this we did get a win on a bitter December night beating them 3-0 in the Semi Final of the J.P.T Southern Area 3-0 with early Kgosi Ntlhe goal added to very late goals from Grant McCann and Nathaniel Mendes Laing our present player Andrew Hughes went off with a hamstring strain and Connor Washington who was to join us later in the season were both in the Exiles line up.

Home win against Bradford City 2-1 at home with Kgosi Ntlhe and Britt Assombalonga on target and on Boxing Day on the short trip to Sixfields to play Coventry City and the team gave the fans no Christmas cheer going down 4-2 also losing at Carlisle United and home to Brentford 3-1over the New Year period. We were given a banana skin drawn in the Third Round of the F.A. to non league Kidderminster Harriers after playing out a goalless draw at Aggborough we slipped on it at London Road losing 3-2 with goals from Tommy Rowe and Britt Assombalonga not being enough and they went on to face Sunderland not a happy hunting ground for the Posh. A 3-0 win at home to Tranmere Rovers with us running up 13 goals without reply in the season with strikes from Britt Assombalonga twice and Nicky Ajose now back after a successful loan spell at Swindon Town who was to net a hat trick in the 4-3 defeat of Nott's County along with Britt Assombalonga.

The next game at the highest point of a ground in the Football league to Oldham Athletic we were to witness in my eyes one of the worse capulations that I have witnessed by a Posh team we were 3-0 up at the break with Britt Assombalonga, Tommy Rowe and Lee Tomblin netting can always remember regular away traveller Alan Tilley saying to me as we were late out after the break perhaps we have declared think we suffered from frost bite from the bitter wind they pulled back two goals and we thought we were safe when Nicky Ajose netted a fourth former Posh player James Wesolowski made it 4-3 Lee Tomlin was shown a red card with two minutes left and our hosts added two in that time to win 5-4 don't think I have used so much bad language addressed at our team soon after we signed Jack Baldwin from Hartlepool's for £500,000, to bolster our leaky defence.

Before the next league game the troubled Lee Tomlin went on loan to Middlesbrough and he was eventually signed permanently to me he was loose cannon but his 132 appearances would have been many more without his much suspension netted 32 goals. But Posh were on our way to Wembley again this time in the Final of the JPT against Swindon Town after two early goals, scored a own goal added to by Kyle Vassall the Robins pulled it back to 2-2 who would think we were only one step from another trip to the home of English football as only just over 3,000 attended the second leg again was very tight with Britt Assomalonga netting before Alex Prichard who had been a very good loan player at London Road levelled thing up and it finally went to penalties and we went through to the final a terrible miss by substitute Tijane put us through, think he was aiming for the renowned Magic Roundabout instead of the goal.

Things were not going well at Leyton Orient before two very late goals from Tommy Rowe and Britt Assombalonga sealed a 2-1 victory the Orient were in third spot and us in sixth little did they know they were going to do battle again at the end of the campaign in the Play Off Semis. The next three saw us only net once with a goalless draw home to Walsall a win at Stevenage with Nicky Ajose on target followed by a 1-0 defeat at Crawley Town on our first league visit to the Checkertrade Stadium. The midweek journey to Sheffield United I think was when we turned up at Hillsborough for this game as Lee our Tourmaster driver had put the wrong post code into his sat-nav but he blamed it on his paperwork we finally arrived and the evening got worse we returned with a 2-0 loss from Bramhall Lane. We managed to get back on the goal trail with a 4-2 home victory over Crewe Alexandra with Britt Assombalonga, Nicky Ajose, Danny Swanson and Connor Washington striking in a 4-2 victory. The short journey to Milton Keynes saw us clock up a victory 2-0 with two early goals from Britt Assombalonga the result left us in 6th place.

The form leading up to the J.P.T final was not good with defeats at home to Rotherham United and away 3-1 to Preston North End. Over 20,000 supported Posh on the journey up the A1 about 15,000 coming out of the woodwork as it was a big game the Posh gave them a day to remember despite Joe Newell being sent off when we were 2-0 up we hung on to win the trophy 3-1 which included first goals for the club for Josh McQuid and Shaun Brisley added to by Britt Assombalonga so more silverware for the Boardroom cabinet. My life was put on hold again as while cleaning the dressing rooms after the 2-0 win against Colchester United on a Tuesday night yes it had to be at the Posh I suffered a slight heart attack I was told and was put in hospital must have been all the excitement of the J.P.T Final.

I had to miss about four games on Doctor's Orders, Sharon Anne was in hospital as well with a bad Urine Infection asked Anne and asked her why I had not come to see her and Anne had to spill the beans that I was in the next ward and she blamed herself for it with all the stress she had put us through Bless her. While I was on sick leave we made the trip to the Wolves and came back empty handed losing 2-0 this result found us in sixth place with the Wolves top of the pile. With a run of only one defeat Bradford City and a last day draw at Port Vale goals at Gillingham through Tommy Rowe and Britt Assombalonga followed by alone Kyosi Ntle last two game saw us assure our playoff spot with wins against Carlisle United again even with the play offs assure the crowd was under 6.000 in a contest which we won 4-1 with a pair from Britt Assombalnga both penalties, Michael Bostwick and Connor Washington and our final away league game at Shrewsbury he scored a pair added to by Lloyd Isgrove and young player on loan from Southampton for run up a 4-2 win and pit us against Leyton Orient in the Play Offs which was going to end in disappointment the first leg played at home ended in a 1-1 draw with a Britt Assombalongo goal with a healthy crowd of over 9.500 the Orient scored after an hour and then added a second with a couple of minutes to play before Connor Washington in the last minute but despite throwing the kitchen sink at them could not level. But to put things in perspective Orient failed at Wembley and now facing life in the National League after 112 years in the Football League only three seasons further on a great club ruined by poor ownership hope the stay in Non League is only brief.

**THE UNDERACHIEVING SEASONS.**

As said at the start of the last chapter not going in any depth the last three season but think we must all agree they have been a great disappointment 2014/5 was our 55th in the Football League and only going to be an average one first ten games produced 19 points we went out of all the Cups very early and had terrible results at Coventry City losing 3-2 after being two up and losing five times at London Road by Christmas the 3-2 loss on Boxing Day but despite this we were still in 5th position. Darren Fergusons reign for the second time at London Road was to end on the 21st February after a dreadful display at Milton Keynes losing 3-0 the team now in free fall in 15th position. Up stepped Youth Academy manager Dave Robertson to take over as caretaker manager and later manager his first four games where all wins the best being the 2-1 defeat away to Sheffield United and at the end of the season he had acquired 22 points in 14 games and lead us to ninth place.

During his spell our world was turned upside down with the loss of Sharon Anne on the 31st March passing away with a stomach haemorrhage not helped by her other health issues he was very supportive to me as saw him most days working at the ground and sent we a nice tweet when I received my award from the Football League a true gentleman you expect your parents to go but not your children to go before me or Anne. She had bounced back so many times but not this one. He did not survive very long into the next season 2015/6 after being sacked after six games then Graham Westley former Stevenage and failed manager at Preston North End took over but he did not last the season out but not before stand in manager Grant McCann had overseen the 5-1 beating of Oldham Athletic he guided the team into play off positions in early January with the 3-2 win at Sheffield United but then went on a run of 11 games without a victory and to my mind picking bizarre teams and said he wanted us to complete 600 passes in a game hardly entertaining when 400 were in our half. Very approachable man who was very good with my young teams having his photo taken with them always had a cuppa in his hand at an away ground my mate Chris Wayte asked him where hers was he went off and brought her one she was very popular on twitter that night when she posted it. With the club in 14th position he was sacked after the defeat at home to Scunthorpe United and we waited for the third appointment in the season perhaps the cause had not been helped by the transfer of Connor Washington to Q.P.R. and signing of three players to replace him.

Grant McCann took over for the last two games both wins against Shrewsbury Town away and Blackpool at home 5-1 and we finished 13th although we had a windfall from the F.A. Cup reaching the Fourth Round going out after a replay and extra time to W.B.A. Shortly after the end of the season Grant McCann was appointed to the manager's role. What did his first season bring obviously a big learning curve some of the players played out of their skin for him and others were very disappointing and under achieved we had horrendous performances at Oldham and Bury which was not fair on the fans who made the long trek. Going to Bolton to see them celebrate promotion and wish it was us. Perhaps our finish in mid table was about right what of next season we need nurture our young players who made the break through at the end of the season, sign a proven goal scorer hopefully we have in Ricky Miller and a keeper and manage to hang on to our other shining youngster even if he is loaned back. We all hope Darragh McAnthony keeps faith with our great club THE POSH.

Well Sharon-Anne that was hard work but was something I wanted to do to all my readers hope you found it interesting hope they find my other chapters on other aspects of the game people who I meet at London Road how the game has changed, Days on the Away Travel, How the stadium has changed and the best and worst players who have worn the Posh Shirt.

# On the Buses with Dot and Olive

As not ever having a car nearly all my away games were travelling on the Away Travel Forever Posh as we have today we have had an array of different companies and now a very good one in Tourmaster. Have lots of stories to tell about my time spent on the road but will not name companies as some are still trading today. My really early days were spent only going by train with my dad. The coaches over the years have on a whole been run by the supporters club but the club did for a spell. The early days when I went the lady in charge of them was the fiery Dot Hennessey and her sidekick Mary, then it was the local dustman Dave Mills, then for a lot of years Yours truly me, and now bless her heart the hard working Forever Posh Chairman Olive alias Chris Wayte. Chris you have often said we could write a book about our experiences on the away travel all you have got is a chapter hope you enjoy it.

In the 60/70s when there were not so many motorways around our trips north used to see our stops coming home at Grantham we used to call either for the fish and chips or for a pint in the pub near the Gingerbreads Grantham Town Fc. Ground think Dot and Mary got a free pint. For trips down South we always called in for a wee stop and Fish and Chips at Baldock this never seemed to change on the way home. In those days we had the same company as the team and we had them for years and usually the same driver. Can't really remember any real incidents as the company did their homework in finding ground but Dot was always in charge, backed up by Mary if we had more than one coach. When Dave the local dustman took over from Dot not a very popular figure with the travellers who had their own name for him but won't print it as he has passed on.

At that time the journey across the Welsh country side to Wrexham sticks out in my memory seeing all the coaches had not seen so many from the club before little did I know that this was only to be humbled by the number we took to Wembley three times and Old Trafford it was a long journey back and the only time I can remember crying at a gamer sitting on the terrace at the Racecourse ground as a goalkeeper Dai Davies the Welsh international broke our hearts saving shots with all parts of his body Wrexham were already champions and Posh had to win to go up to Division 2 in the crowd were a big contingent of Preston fans and they were ecstatic as we were heartbroken when the game finishing 0-0 and saw them promoted can remember Barry Butlin missing an open goal but the damaged had been done the game before when we lost 4-3 at Chester with Alan Slough scoring a hat trick of penalties some very dubious courtesy of referee Mr Newcombe for us. For some reason we changed the coach company and this is where the fun or stress started.

One Bank Holiday before mobile phones I can remember waiting very early for a coach to take us for a 3pm kick off again to Wrexham when it did not arrive, phoned the firms garage at Cambridge to be told they thought it was an evening kick off, by chance the driver who was taking us was in the yard and he broke all records to get us to game with 20 minutes to spare. Another fruitless journey to Sheffield United at the end of the 1981/2 season as we went on a terrible run at the death and as we had three games in five days, when it came to the trip which many had bought tickets for game which was made all ticket and bought well in advance it was a nothing game and Posh lost 4-0 at the hands of the Champions.

Another company took us to Tottenham in the mid nineties for a FA cup replay we had a convoy of coaches with a group turning up very late who had spent the day in the pub obviously they happened to be on the coach my dear daughter Sharon Anne was looking after. When we arrived at Tottenham the driver told me this group had been very suggestive and rude to her and he would not be taking them back. After the game which we lost on penalties, with young Andy Furnell missing from the spot. I decided to go back on Sharon's coach as knew there would be trouble, we got the passengers on very quickly and as we shut the doors this group arrived tried to force their way on with lots of threats, we know where you live, we are going to torch your car little did they know I have never driven. We drove with them banging on the coach hope they had the money to get home from Kings Cross.

On reflection on my last visit, previously to White Hart Lane I was dumped at then by a girl of my dreams not a happy ground for me. The group was picked out by our then Football Police Liaison officer Johnny Harlock and he paid them a visit later in the week. I have been involved with in two exoduses to Wembley were all our fans come out of the woodwork taking 25-30 coaches bring them in from all over the county and beyond the trip in 1999/0 nearly beaten by the elements and saw players aqua planning across the turf and also playing havoc with some of the old coaches I stood in the pouring rain until the last coach arrived with 15 minutes to spare till kick off time. Perhaps the stand out game was the journey to Huddersfield's old Leeds Road ground and our playoff game the celebrations afterwards were awesome you could get so close to the players not like at Wembley Another game that springs to mind is the was the trip to non league Dagenham in the FA Cup First Round when luckily we had none of our passengers injured when the away end wall collapsed the same as Posh losing 1-0.

A trip to Shrewsbury's old Gay Meadow not anything to do with the two 2-0 loss saw a bit of club history in the making with us being drawn at home to the mighty Liverpool which we saw of via a Gary Kimble cross that floated into the top corner reach the Fifth Round of the Rumbelows Cup and a long journey took us to Middlesbrough in a replay which was postponed at short notice by referee Mr Hackett meaning that all the coaches were turned round at Hartshead Moor Services near Huddersfield he did not figure on their Xmas card next year but our club paid for the fans travel who had made the journey for re arranged date which saw us go down to a single goal.

At this time Sharon Anne was very friendly with the wayward Gary Cooper and he would always look after her with away tickets and was shocked one day when a fan came asking how was the baby thinking that Sharon Anne was his partner also a trip to Millwall become a very long journey home she being ribbed as Chris Greenman who she was very friendly with put through his own goal and Posh lost 1-0That season when the votes for Evening Telegraph Player of the Season were cast he ran a very close second to Steve Welsh think she got all her mates to vote for Chris as he was no great player.

Another memory is going to Charlton at the end of the 1992-3 season which saw us relegated from the Championship next to me and Sharon Anne sat a very smartly dressed man who was asking us about the club and players did not help Scott Cookseys cause as he had his usual night mare and we went down 5-1 at the start of the next season it turned out to be our next manager John Still and he recognised us. Trouble with the coach companies carried on even though we switched them many times we had a saga of a journey to Cheltenham a ground which we had not been to before, dear old Brenda who is no longer with us said she had relatives in the area and she knew a better way to the ground she got us hopelessly lost and on turning round in a gateway and finished up in a ditch we tried pushing but with a 52 seated coach you stand no chance so we tried digging out, putting boards under the wheels, but to no avail we managed to get hold of the other coach which had now arrived at the ground and it picked up all our passengers and took them on to the game. Eventually the driver managed to free the coach with help of a local tractor but not before the company had sent a replacement from Nottingham needless to say we never let her be our navigator again bless her.

Other classics were a coach on the way to Stoke bursting an air bag and we were stranded in middle lane of the motorway which was not to liking of the local Police and thought they were going to take our driver away but Ginge my old mate now Chief Scout at Cambridge Unite saved the day as his Junior Posh coach had reached the ground and they picked us all up and saved the day. We turned up to go to Macclesfield a very undulating journey we were greeted with an old double decked bus from the ark driver by a very old Noah complete with ticket machine we were all exhausted when we got there pedalling up those hills. With the same company we had a double Decker go all the way to Oxford at about 30mph when the driver had trouble with his gears think we spend half the journey on the hard shoulder another one nearly deposited me in the River Nene from the crew seat when we went over the Town Bridge and the coach doors flew open.

One the most embarrassing incidents was when I was called to the back of the bus on a journey when a young lad had a fit made him comfortable cleared the back seat to my surprise his girlfriend touched him between the legs and said as least he has not wet himself I needed to put him in the recovery position but no way was I going to remove his head from her buxom breasts so called to Chris Wayte to do the honours. Another medical emergency was when Geordie Balmer Sharon used to call him her adopted Granddad and always used to sit with him on the front seat of the coaches we were playing at Leyton Orient on a bitter winter evening and he returned to the coach very disorientated cold and looked terrible we managed to go back to the stadium and the club doctor looked him over by that time we had mobile phones and phoned his daughter and managed to get her pick him up on our return to London Road. I have never been so worried on a journey we thought he was going to die on us. He returned to enjoy many more away days before he passed away and told many old tales about players and football. Have had many characters on the travel over the years Mr and Mrs Dunham who travelled with us many years did not bring a pack up they brought a picnic hamper complete with table cloth and serviettes we also had a man won't say gentleman who's language to say the least was very blue and did not mince his words even with ladies on the coach on the way home from a game a cry comes from him at the back of the where's my fxxxxxx stick and hat previous to this driver had to go and shut the emergency door where he was sitting and they were now perhaps sitting on the Motorway he wanted us to go back and look for them of course we did no one would have been brave enough to hide them he was built like Big Daddy the old wrestler.

When the Big Ron television programme about Barry Fry was being filmed we were lucky not to be reported to the police as we did about six takes going round the old Ferrybridge services roundabout.

A trip to Cardiff saw us pelted with coins in the ground the week after a pitch battle the game before against Leeds United and escorted after the no not by Police motor bikes but by two police horses of all things and they left us in the middle of nowhere and we finished going back the way we had come and took our lives in our own hands. The final straw come with a company now out of business the coach arrived and we started loading when somebody shouted there's not enough seats Chris thought they meant people were saying them could not sit together on checking we were six seats short they had been taken out for wheelchair booking the day before and not put back and the driver had not checked we found another set in the boot and had to wait while the others arrived from the companies garage then the driver gave us a tour of Bristol trying to find the ground and then we got beat.

Just coming out of Blackpool on a trip we had to take evasive action when a lorry perhaps doing a moon light flit in daylight deposited somebody's worldly goods in front of the coach. Another trip saw us on our hands and knees looking for an elusive pair of false teeth which poor old Brenda Collison had supposedly lost bless her after about ten minutes she found them in her hand she had taken them out to eat! Brenda you were a hero and again left us with many pleasant memories especially about the lovely bright lights of the city when we come back from a long journey along the A605 as was her best friend Jenny Brown who like Brenda went all over country on the coaches.

Recently we have had a Coach Hopper a foreign man turned up while we were loading at the ground to go to Port Vale he asked Chris is we had any vacant seats she made it very clear as we had not seen him before the coach was going to football at Port Vale which he seemed to understand she told him it would be £21 he sat down thinking that he would bring the money to her when we got to the M6 toll services she was going to ask him again I saw him talking to another coach asking him if he was going to Manchester needless to say we left him at the service he had a means to an end we wont be doing that again. As I said before we had very few hick-ups with our current company although took time out after Sharon became very ill from travelling away, the two that come to mind are both about our regular driver Lee first turning up last season going to Sheffield finishing up at Hillsborough when we were actually playing at Bramhall Lane blamed it on his sat nav but he put in the post code, and him looking forward to his fish and chips at Rochdale when we were on the journey to Bury Recently on our trip to Chelsea travelled on Tourmasters new double decked coach which nearly used all the profit that Posh would make on the game a couple of weeks after a car ran into the back of it. On the journeys home if we have lost we have 52 passengers all with different opinions of the games, players, formation, officials and the manager but we are not going to change the result. But hopefully we will there at the next game even if its Plymouth, Milton Keynes or Cobblers getting behind the team we love THE POSH.

# How the game has changed in 60 years of watching the Posh

Well the ball is still round and we still play on grass at least in the Football league and at London Road sorry the Abax Stadium we used to play the ball forward from the kick off now that's changed to a pass back then all the way back to the keeper who used to pick the ball up from one of his team mates passes, then he could bounce it around and punt it up field in his toe capped boots not like the carpet slippers they wear today and all the pretty colours, not conventional coloured shirts red, blue or white now wear colours like at London Road recently with away strips being Cherry Volt and this season luminous yellow which confused Michael Boswick at the Cobblers. This season another stand out one was, Mick Vincent's Pizza shirts we have worn at Posh.

    The ball is now so light keepers can kick from one end of pitch to the other a bit different to the old leather ball we used to play with as I did in local football complete with lace which left a in print on your forehead and knocked you into next week if you were brave enough to head on a wet day and it was heavy as an old medicine ball you had in the old school gyms.

    I don't think much has changed on the pitches only today players play mostly on billiard tables instead of the old mud baths covered in sand which were played on every Sat with First Team and Reserves and perhaps mid week games as well. Pitches are now covered if weather if threatening no under soil heating at Posh only hessian covers that take only minus 3 degrees perhaps we should have told that to the groundsman at Oldham after our fruitless three hour journey to Oldham this season. But that proves that they are the most undervalued people at a club especially with the pitch Dan Selcraig has nursed at London Road this term they get it wrong at you don't get a game with the criteria the officials have to take in consideration in a game that in my opinion has gone soft. Long gone are the days of the heavy roller and teams in the Premier have special rows of light to aid the growth of the grass. Years ago pitches in the local leagues used to be marked out with creosote but elf and safety but an end to that.

    Kits have changed immensely not just the different colours all clubs now have home kits, away kits and a third one bet mums and dads love that and all the other merchandise we have in the club shop, it used to be bobble hats, metal badges, scarves and rosettes and the kits change each season. Sponsors for the shirts came in the 80s when Sodastream was the club's first shirt sponsor now firms can now bring their staff for a jolly to sponsor the match ball, programme, game be the shirt sponsor have an advertising board at the ground or for the very rich people or firms you can have an Executive Box for £11,000 plus vat for 12 people. Or your little lad can be mascot for just under £300. A bit different to when the club had the Posh Pool, run by the Supporters Club and Cantwells Crusade and bucket collections to keep us afloat plus local firms sponsoring the match ball.

I hate to think how the rules have changed for offside now you need a manual and a slide ruler in some of the televised games keepers now have to be contortionists as they can't use their hands for a back pass to them now they have to be as good with their feet as on field players. Now fouls are given for the slightest of could you call offences but one horrible thing that has come into the game in the later years is the use of the elbow by players which can cause horrific cuts etc, the likes of Norman Rigby and Co would be sent off every game for sliding and block tackles etc and dear Tommy Robson would go for simulation or falling over before half time when he started his dive at Moy's Lane End and finished in front of the number 305 bus in Bridge Street but he used to get us a lot of penalties conning the referees, a job I would not do for all the tea in Boston harbour however they try they cannot please everybody and are usually the most hated person at a game yes they are well paid mostly in our division they are part time and have a day job if you get two games in a week it's a good windfall.

The person I really feel sorry for is the poor Fourth Official another change that how come in the later years if the officials got injured the PA announcer said if there is a referee in the ground could he report to the tunnel and they found him some kit now we have to find a fourth official if one of the referees team get injured and can't hold up the board for Fergie time or the numerous substitution teams make for formations, injury or to slow the game down when under pressure some in Fergie time he gets the wrath of the managers and the numerous bench when his boss makes a decision that don't go there teams way.

They now arrive at the ground looking as if they are going for a week away with all the different outfits they wear only all black years ago in that era we had some characters in the middle how many old fans can remember Mr Fussey from Retford who was fitter than the players with his sprinting, Smiller

Tommy Dawes from Norwich, Alf Grey from Yarmouth and a bit later on Roger Fitzpatrick think from Leicester and Ray Lewis yes from Great Bookham in Surrey and also Mr Coddington who was knocked over by Mr Blobby and also remember our own local Football league referee Bruce Buckle who lived in Wharf Road where my junior school St.Augustines was.

They are now under a lot more pressure with the rules that seem to change every season with all the officials being watched by an assessor now changed to an observer this season at the games and in the Premiership you have ex referrers like Graham Poll or Howard Webb giving their verdicts on them in the newspapers or on the television which I don't agree with they have a split second to make a decision either rightly or wrongly we as fans hope they level out over 46 games now being sponsored by Gillette shaving foam which players rub out before the free kicks are taken. What about the benches we now have seven substitutes teams can pick from, Manager, Assistant Manager, Goal keeping Coach, Physio used to be called Trainer, Fitness Coach,Massuer, Kit Man and Water Carrier in the 60/70 years used to be one substitute if the keeper got injured an on field player had to don the shirt also on the bench were only the manager and trainer if it was Bill Harvey sprinting on they soon got up quick with his cold sponge not like today when they go down as though they have shot with the magic sprays they use, we now have young lady trainers they are not so quick getting up, and the ball boy who doubled up as half time scoreboard boy done for years by my friend Bunny Eglin.

Teams now have such big squads at Posh at Senior level we have the League team and the Reserve team that plays a limited number of games at the Training ground when we in the Football Combination later to become the London Combination we had a game at London Road every Saturday and on top of that we had a team in the United Counties and the Peterborough League – players used to be numbered one to 11 now with the Premiership it will soon be 1-100 how is the fourth offial going to cope with that Chelsea have 39 players out on loan this season the best loan players we have at London Road in recent years think have been George Thorne, keeper Lee Harrison, Alex Prichard and at present Luke McGee.

What has happened to the Smiths and Jones in all our league teams without any English sounding names the match announcers can't pronounce not that it will bother our fans one told me they have not a word he is saying for years anyway due to our PA system. One of my pet hates is all the stewards we have to have on Saturdays we have nearly a hundred at the ground and when a local derby backed up by the law. Years ago we had a bobby in each corner who would

## The Posh Affair 111

patrol round the running track and ask us kids to put our legs back over the wall but to no avail when he moved on we put them back over again, and in the stand we had stewards in long white coats showing people to their seats. Wages are now obscene in the top divisions can remember when players got summer wages and had part time jobs.

Teams no longer travel on the day of the match but in a luxury coach unless it's very near they stay in hotels overnight and if not they have a pre match bite wonder how many times my mate Tommy Robson did this in his 500 odd games but he was spoilt when we had his favourite sponsor in his career when Wells Ales were our shirt sponsors for one season think the lads drunk all the profits on a day at the Brewery they never renewed the next season much to the players disgust. We now have love in when a player scores and the scorer disappears in a scrum of teammates and do silly dances what has happened to the old fashioned hand shake of years ago.

Keepers now wear gloves like wicket keepers in cricket and even wear them for training and warm ups they only used to wear them if it was wet and now he have on field players wearing them and officials as well. They now also wear short sleeved jerseys good job they don't play on council pitch. When I first first went to a game keepers used to roll necked jerseys like fishermen Can remember years ago Keith Weller playing for Leicester City in tights. No wonder we get such small gates you only have to see why at the Railway station on match days and see all the local people going off to watch their adopted teams mostly, off to watch a London based team, Norwich, Leicester or Nottingham Forest. Our Chairman does like to keep the prices down but don't think he realises that most people in city are on the minimum wage or work for agency firms where their hours are not assured and football comes a long way along their wish list especially if they have a family and now if you can afford it you can watch a game nearly every night on Sky or BT Sport.

A club can offer only minimum of offers to the non ticket holders as it's likely to upset the Season Ticket holders who have paid up front and kept the clubs afloat in the close season. Players now wear things like bras under the shirts when training and playing to monitor the players performance and fatigue so a player cannot hide during a game as it shows on his monitor and to the benches these could be sponsored by Abax sorry they only do transport and also monitored for amount of fluid they take on during the game don't think they now have a cuppa or a slice of orange at half the top up with the supplement drinks.

Teams all had Youth teams but that only meant training a couple of nights and a game on a Saturday now we have at Posh like all league clubs and many non league clubs an academy where players spread time time between that and schooling wonder if clubs get the expected number of lads to come through to be full time players for the outlay that they spend or firms sponsoring the acamedys.How the FA Cup and the League Cup has been devalued by the top clubs now playing mainly reserve teams until they get to the Semi Final stages and then the reserve players are put out to grass and if they win it they perhaps don't receive a medal.

In the 50/60 we used to get fined by the Northants FA if we fielded an under strength side think we got fined a £100 one season and that was a lot of dosh. What a brain wave from the EFL with the Checkertrade Trophy competition the Freightrover, Johnstone Paint Trophy were bad enough but gave 20,000 or so fans who came out of the woodwork a good day out at Wembley among the 200 who made the trip to Newport in an earlier round for a night game must have been such an embarrassment with the gates and pictures in the Non League Paper of a stand at Fleetwood with four supporters and two stewards who don't do it for free starring in it.

Now we go to new stadiums every season with all fancy names of mostly sponsors long gone are the quaint grounds like Gay Meadow at Shrewsbury and the run down Layer Road at Colchester or the Cricket County ground at the Cobblers but still look at London Road as a proper football ground as former Premiership referee Dermot Gallagher said me when assessing the officials at the stadium recently to me. Owners of clubs are now changing every season with over 20 foreign owners in the EFL and it worries me if Darragh who bank rolls our club pulls the plug we would finish up like old county rivals Rushden and Diamonds now reformed as AFC Rushden and Diamonds with their old ground now demolished and ground sharing the same as Kettering Town and in the demise of Leyton Orient this campaign, the loved by me or hated by others Barry Fry won't keep us afloat again.

I would feel more at ease if we had a board of directors as in days gone by all putting their money in not one main man. Another thing we all used to do was the pools either Littlewoods, Vernon's or Zetters and we had collectors who came door to door or collectors at work now we can even bet on line even at Reserve games as I found out this season watching our lads and you can now cash out before the game has finished bet on goal scorers even corners. Another thing that came about in 1981 was the three points for a win previous to that it was two points for a victory very good if you on a winning run if not gaps appear very quickly and you are soon in free fall. Also we had the play offs come into being in 1987 so teams season can last a bit longer than the old format and bring lots of revenue in to the clubs coffers. The play offs have been very successful for us since being introduced and now clubs get parachute payments when relegated.

Now try and name all the managers of clubs in the League something perhaps that you could do twenty years ago but with three managers gone in the week of writing this piece and some clubs going through five a season you don't stand a chance of naming them and half of them in the Premier don't speak good English perhaps that's because they are all foreign. Games are now played on any old day of the week to help the coffers of the television companies even on what used to be the sacred day of Sundays then you went to Sunday school in the morning and not allowed down the passage in the afternoon to play in the street. We used to talk about wages and transfer fees in pounds then thousands and now in multi millions little wonder that some players go off the rails and the end of their playing careers if they have not invested it during their playing days. Times have moved on has the beautiful game got any better I reserve judgement as perhaps many others from my era. As my wife Anne says it's only a game.

**THE GOOD THE BAD AND THE UGLY**

In the sixty years wonder how many players I have seen play for the club some have made a good impression, some can't remember, some were useless and by their sell by dates and some were ugly in the nature of their game.

Have tried to compile a list of the sixty best players that I have seen over the last sixty years of watching my beloved team have only included one present player who to me is a legend at the club still going strong at 40. This is saying that any of them are not good enough but most are young and still learning there trade. The list took a long while to compile sure have missed players out sure some oldies like me will let me know,

**MY DIAMOND ANNIVERSARY LIST.**

Tony Adcock, Britt Assombalonga, Ian Bennett, Ryan Bennett, Terry Bly, George Boyd, Jack Carmichael, Ollie Conmy, Robbie Cooke, John Cozens, Ian Crawford, Vic Crowe, Simon Davies, Derek Dougan, Bobby Doyle, Adam Drury, Dennis Emery, Matthew Etherington, Marcus Ebdon, David Farrell, Mick Gynn, Dwight Gayle, Mick Gooding, David Gregory, Mick Jones, Ollie Hopkins, Jim Hall Billy Hails, Mick Halsall, Freddie Hill, Billy Kellock, Noel Luke, Charlie Lee, Craig MacKail-Smith, Russell Martin, Gerry McElhinney, Leon McKenzie, Grant McCann, Peter McNamee,.Aaron McLean, Tony Millington, Frank Noble, Tommy Rowe, Norman Rigby, Alan Slough, Peter Price Trevor Quow, Frank Rankmore, Keith Ripley, Tommy Robson, David Robinson, Trevor Slack, Worrell Stirling, Lee Tomblin, Mark Tyler, Chris Turner, Keith Waugh, Steve Welsh, David Seaman and Gabriel Zakuani.

Very difficult to pick a top 10 but this is my selection

1. Freddie Hill best £5,000 the club ever spent way back in the middle seventies. Magic with free kicks
2. Tommy Robson we always fall out as I tell my tours he is the runner up always says the club made a convience of him his Legends photo in the Family Stand is between two toilet doors say no more.
3. Chris Turner a legend served the club in all capacities true gent great player soon to be remembered by his statue outside the Main Stand.
4. Mark Tyler Can remember his debut with Birmingham putting four by him a great legend at the club looks now that his playing career has come to an end great keeper and sure is a good coach.

5   George Boyd Still going well in the Premiership with Burnley pure genius in his Posh career bet his barber has gone out of business.

6   Mick Halsall Skipper of the first Wembley triumph a great leader you would rather be in his team than playing against him. Now coach at the Abbey Stadium.

7   David Seaman Best things Martin Wilkinson did as manager was bring him from Leeds United went to make 75 appearances for England and over 400 games for Arsenal.

8   Jim Hall Old fashion centre forward never knocked off the ball vital player in the 1973-4 Fourth Division Championship side. Holds the club goal scoring record of Football League goals.

9   Jack Carmichael Very rugged full back would have spent lots of time suspended with today's soft set of rules etc. Popular member again of the 1973-4 winning side after leaving the club had a spell in the maturing American Soccer League where he now lives.

10  Ken Charley Club hero with his goals at Huddersfield Town in the Semi Final and Final in 1991/2 seen holding the Barclays trophy does anybody know where it is Bob Burrows keeps looking on E bay for it.

**THE BAD**

Although we have had many good players in my sixty years have seen players who have come to be club some with good records elsewhere but were complete flops here some that spring to mind are Howard Forinton signed by Barry Fry from Birmingham City for £250,000 lot of money as he had only played five games for them and only made 50 for us scoring 10 goals. Bill Green joined from West Ham in 1978/9 season for £60,000 only managed 30 average games for us very disappointing. Carl Griffith was signed from Portsmouth for a club record in 1995/6 season for £225,000 scored on two minutes on his debut his only strike in 16 games and was sold on to Leyton Orient for £65,000.in more recent times we have had Tyrone Barnett who we signed for over a million from Crawley Town they must have seen us coming then we took a big hit when Shrewsbury Town paid just over £100,000 in 2015 and Luke James who we signed from Hartlepool's United in 2014 for £500,000 who could not find the net only netting twice in 30 odd gates despite trying so hard now on a season loan to Bristol Rovers. Some of the oldies on the coach go on about Harry Holman being the worst player they have seen in Posh colours he came from

Exeter City must have been bad can't remember him. But can remember David Rogers who came on loan from Partick Thistle he was hauled off in his debut at Luton Town after we went 2-0 down in the first twelve minutes and he did not appear after the break he kept looking at his boots a poor work man blames his tools they say. The same fate happened to Nazgi Kuqi signed in 2005/6 season on loan from Birmingham City he had a bath at half time in his debut and never appeared in a Posh shirt again. He has had some good keepers but a few dodgy ones Scott Cooksey, Joe Neenan and John Keeley spring to mind. In the seventies we signed a lot of players by their sell by dates Eddie Clamp, Nigel Simms, Peter McParland, Billy Day and Jack Overfield spring to mind and who can forget keeper Dick Beattie who certainly was a bad man with throwing games.

**THE UGLY**

Fred Barber must be at the top of the list with his old man's mask wearing it for the warm up and presentation to the sponsors etc at Wembley against Stockport County we thought he was still wearing it when he allowed the giant Kevin Francis to score through his error. Ray H ankin was another ugly player finally getting the sack because of persistent indiscipline on the field after clocking up five early baths in a season. Times have moved on wonder what today's referees would think too hard and sometimes ugly tackling of the seventies by the likes of Norman Rigby, Ollie Hopkins, Keith Ripley to name a few and later on the Micky Halsalls, Steve Welsh and two footed tackles by Marcus Ebdon and the take no prisoners policy of Guy Branston today's referees would have had a field day and they would been for even suspended.

# From London Road to the Abax

As we all know the name of the stadium was changed from the original London Road ground or stadium to the Abax Stadium when they bought the title in 2014 on a five year lease but to me Posh always play at London Road. Will not go over the history of the ground from day one as contour y to some people think I was not around then only own it has changed in sixty years that I can remember. A trip to London Road in the late fifties with day would take us down Orchard Street down Queens Walk past Fletton Towers with Miss Hartley's Wolfhounds in the grounds over the Peacock Bridge then with steam trains running under it across Fletton Avenue into Glebe Road to make our way through the iron turnstiles to take our places on the terrace on old railway sleepers if the day was wet we all headed for the ramshackle old stand which used to stand at the Moy's Lane end of the terrace. But in those days you could move from end to end to which way we were kicking the exception being the old wooden grandstand which my father remembered being built in 1923. Coming from the town side of the bridge you could catch the 305 bus and get off at the ground or a walk which would take you over the River Nene over the East Station Bridge yes we had two stations you could catch a train from the North Station to the East Station then past Mr Pugs leys Tobacconist shop with the aroma of it as you walked by or called in to buy a packed of his broken crisps think they were the sweepings of the factory floor but they tasted all right to us youngsters.

    The Royal Oak public house on the corner of London Road kept many years by Phillip Strickland of the Peterborough and County F.A. was the fans watering hole in later years called Port out Starboard Home spelling POSH but nothing to do with the clubs nickname then cut across the car park which the team trained on if the weather was bad not so many cars about in those days but we had a policeman standing in his box directing the traffic out after the game and then either take your place if rich sitting down in the main stand with the team running out to the strains of Post Horn Gallop and Dusty ringing his bell and going round with his half time competion board don't think he went to the grammar school results or standing under cover at London Road End but think when I started going that the Moy's Lane named after the Moy's Railway Wagon Works behind the stand was partly covered as well. The sides of the ground was surrounded by a white or it was originally by a wooden fence but behind the goals we had the concrete walls can remember the wooden tea huts behind the stand think the one at London Road is still in the same place and the one at Moy's Lane End run by the Supporters Club who it was reported had over 40,000 members in 1956 a bit different to today's membership.

We used to collect all the empty glass pop bottles up after the game and get the three pence deposit on them. Plans for a new main Grandstand it turns out were submitted in 1948 this was to be 4,000 capacity bringing the ground capacity up to 25,000 but were deferred many times and not started till 1955 and completed for the start of the 1958/9 season while that was being built the players came out on running boards as the pitch had been moved over.

Floodlights were the next thing on the agenda one set in each corner we still have the old tower at London Road Main Stand corner which will go if the end is developed at a future date. They were opened when Arsenal were the visitors in February 1960 in a 1-1 draw Posh had a series of these games against top opposing sides. One of the next projects was the full covering of both ends and the terracing on Gleb e Road with four executive boxes and later a TV gantry in case Sky popped in. This made it easier for teams to kick the ball in the dying minutes if holding for a result clearing the back terrace wall and finishing up in Billy Hails garden in Glebe Road referees where not so keen on Fergie time in this era and players did not seem to take the ball in the corners like today's game to waste time.

As the wall at the back not a lip on it and if caught out on a wet day you could get some shelter under it and collect a pile of bricks to see over the perimeter wall at the front can you imagine that happening today the Championship sorry First Division then in 1992 when they had to raise their seating capacity under the Taylor report and it saw the Main Stand enclosure changed from standing to seating again money was tight and the club purchased 700 seats from the old Filbert Street stadium at Leicester when they moved and a further 300 complete from Millwall in the close season. Also the offices were upgraded, hospitality areas improved, The Posh Pub added and a small club shop.

Due to the bigger crowds usually swelled by the opposition supporters the club with help from the Football League for funds to erect a two tier stand to replace the Glebe Road terracing but not before an outcry by the residents' of the area and it took a march from the ground by fans headed by CEO Chris Turner to the Town Hall for the City Council to give it the green light. The stand was going to hold 5,000 fans and was finally opened with a boring goalless game against Blackpool in late March 1996 not the start of the New Year as the club had promised. Funny that the last game the terrace was used was again against the same opponents resulting in a 1-0 win with David Farrell scoring did we really want the new stand the gate was only 5,716 but we were looking ahead to greater things...

Next up was the replacement of the old floodlights and now we had low level ones for the start of the 2012/13 season. The final bit of the jig saw to date was the erection of the Motor point stand on the dated Moy's Lane End terracing site having been plastered on the back wall of it many times when we held shooting practise on the floodlight car park where we used to train with my club Stanground United no 3G pitches then it was tarmac. The new stand was first used for the League for the visit of Swindon Town who turned us over 2-1 with ex manager Mark Cooper in charge of them. The gate was over 7,000 and 1,700 Posh fans used the new facility which holds 2,602 fans but now for most games half of it is closed to save on expenses like stewarding etc as not warranted with the poor gates that we get. The stand was built by the Peterborough City Council. Who now use it for offices and a Future Business centre and it is also is the home of our stadium sponsors offices as well who have signed up till 2019.

The ground Certificated capacity is now 14,084 Family stand 4,416, Main Stand 4,999, Motorpoint 2,602 and London Road Terracing 2,669 less segregation. What of the future of London Road we all know if we get promoted we have to have an all seater stadium either rebuilding or the cheap option of fixing seats to the existing terrace will we ever have a new stadium? They have a lot to offer take the likes of Doncaster and Rotherham which I think are the best I have seen in the lower leagues. Does it warrant it with the gates we get personally with spending a lifetime at London Road hope the rest of my days are spent at London Road or the ABAX stadium still a genuine football ground.

# Posh People

Over my sixty years' have meet and have lots of memories of people who are still with us and ones who have unfortunate passed away the made a great impression with me and sure lots of posh fans.

Chris Wayte The hardworking Chairperson of our Official Supporters Club Forever Posh who has gone through very worrying times recently with her treatment for cancer. Served under lots of different Chair people like me before she took over the reins. Had some good times with her on the Away travel think the highlight was when she nearly caused an accident as Alan our usual number two couch driver passed us on a trip and she gave us a flash lifting up her top he has never been the same since. Also some worrying times when part of our committee wanted to take Barry Fry to court back in the Peter Boizot days. Has been a good soul mate of mine for now over 30 years.

Bob Burrows The genial board room host on Match days at London Road sorry the Abax Stadium who knows most people in football including the Pope and who does not know him in our city with his days as a Milkman heaven knows how we got his round done h e speaks for England our it should be Ireland, fish and chip man, Junior football manager at Woodston Dynamos, Church worker who he used to bless any person who was ill from his own church community or the Posh one including my own Sharon on air when he used to act as summariser for Posh games on Cambridgeshire and in earlier days on hospital radio. Long may his stories continue and his blessings to all who visit the boardroom. Was rewarded with his service to the club at the clubs Awards night this season well deserved. God bless You

Bill Harvey Sadly no longer with us passed away in 2002 was manager at Luton Town and Grimsby Town joining the Posh as Physio, Coach and Youth team manager joining the club in 1981 and served it till retiring after the first Wembley win in 1990-1. The crowd used to cheer him when he raced on to the pitch at London Road pitch and players used to make a very quick recovery with his magic sponge and potions. In 1987 he was so proud to an award from the Football League Executive Staff for his Services to Football. We was a great friend to us as a family and a great help with physio for our Sharon when she had her first disease Dystonia which contorts your muscles and used to always find time often surrounded with dirty kit from the games on a Sunday and always Uncle Bill had a special in her heart and us as a family in ours as well. A great man.

Margaret and Derek Poole Mr and Mrs Peterborough United many fans used to call them when they both worked at the ground for about 30 odd years. It was so sad when Derek recently passed away after serving the club in many different jobs starting working in the Commercial and Lottery Dept under an another old servant of the club Ellis Stafford who received a very belated 1960-1 medal from the FA as being part of Fourth Division Championship side, then the job of grounds man came up and Derek took it he was self taught and then went on to get all his qualifications in a job he did for a lifetime of seasons. Worked with him a number of seasons on match days on the pitch often getting early morning phone calls or Friday night calls when the game was in doubt or we had the covers on several times in at six in the morning clearing snow and very grateful to him when Sharon Anne had her strokes gave up all of my jobs at the club it was him who got we back me back when my life was on hold. Later Derek moved indoors to be Darren Fergusons kit man a job he loved and took a great pride in. The only part of it he did not like where the overnight stays when he was away from his beloved Margaret she said it was the only time they had been apart and she had to have the lights on when he was away. Margaret still watches the home games and goes to some of the near away games. What great servants to the club and what a great pair they were together.

Barry Fry The man you hear in the offices at the ground before you see him still calls he mate at the ground after about 20 years of being around still don't think he knows my name. Still we hear supporters which now are perhaps followers saying they are not going why he is at the club. My own view is that without him and his investment in the club before Daragh McAnthony came along we could have been a piece of barren land like Rushden and Diamonds Nene Park or London Road could have been built on and hopefully a phoenix club formed and ground sharing with Northern Star or Peterborough Sports like AFC Rushden and Diamonds. His wheeling and dealing has kept the club in business since Daragh came on the scene. With our gates we are always going to be a selling club. Here's hoping he can find the club some more gems to sell on in years to come. As we all know very straight talking with a good vocabulary of works beginning with the letter F. When asked recently at the club A.GM. If it was true that Daragh not been asked to sell the club to a foreign buyer his answer was its load of old bxxxxxxs. Say no more.

Graham Gobber Linford Same can be said of him as Barry Fry you can hear him miles away so anybody who has not come across you know where he got his nickname. Has been a regular home and away supporter and travelled on the away travel as long as I can remember flogging his Posh lottery tickets with his patter only four for a pound or twenty for a fiver and never gives small winners you always have to have your winnings in tickets at the end of the season when Chris Abbot had a £50 winner after at first trying him to have his winnings in tickets had to borrow money off his friends yes he has some to pay the winnings in cash. Tells me his first game was in 1964 and his favourite players of all time are Jim Hall, Bobby Doyle and keeper Keith Waugh. He is very proud to be a PE 1 supporter and calls all of our of town supporters swampies was going to Yarmouth every week to see his young lady but now she lives with him. Hope he gives us plenty of time for a collection on the coach so you don't have to get wed in your jeans.

Adi Mowles The man at the helm of the Posh Independent Supporters Club or PISA which think was formed as an alternative to get shut of Barrie Fry many years ago but in that respect Ali you have to admit you have failed as he is still around the club but not as manager as he was in those days. Always very outspoken which often gets him in trouble remember at Wycombe Wanderers a few years ago when he stepped over the small wall and gave there keeper a hand getting the ball back in play a bit quicker in injury time which was not appreciated and did not see the end of the game. Over the many years we have known each other we have had many spats or heated opposite opinions. You either love him or hate him Adi I sit on the fence. But one thing you can say about him you cannot fault his passion for the POSH

Daragh McAnthony Don't know much about him only that his money keeps the club in business which we are all grateful for but he must be very frustrated with the falling attendances but people will only come through the turnstiles to see a winning side especially in our city. But taking on a First Division side is not going to make you money. Wish he was more fan friendly but spends lots of time out of the country but sees all games as they are beamed to him like him stand on the terraces now and again instead of breezing through to the directors box and have more contact with the Supporters Group committees especially with Forever Posh the Official Supporters Club but I am biased and my young groups who come to the match surely our fans of the future which numbered over 100 teams last season and brought just short of £30,000 into the club. Perhaps when he reads this I will be out of a job and loose my pocket money.

The Green family Roy was a very good supporter of my charity work in running marathons and later long distance walks no good asking him to sponsor me with money it was what do you want on my Macmillan Way Walk from Boston to Abbotsbury in Dorset about 300 miles remember saying a good pair of walking boots at £70 no problem purchase them. He was a regular at London Road before sadly passing away but Emma says he only took her to one away match at Brighton when Gill could not go. He did lots of work when Joanie's challenge upgraded the home dressing room for free and know every time Gill goes on a dressing room tour she looks at the plaque on the tunnel wall very proudly. As we all know Emma works as Retail Manager at the club and both her and Gill travel on the coaches and are members of the Forever Posh Committee. A true POSH family

Mick Robinson The man I hate having with sponsors on my ground tours what he don't know about the club if not worth knowing. His books about the club I am sure like I found a great read he can be found at every game home and away although he does not do friendliest he tells me. Very surprised when he actually asked me if the club had a keeper captain before Ben Anwick don't think we had unless Jack Fairbrother or George Swindon did it in the Midland league days any more takers for a answer. If you see Mick you know his sidekicks Nigel Cowling who comes from Bradford every game and Mick Sexton who again have known for years. Congratulations many times commiserations to him for just clocking up 900 games on the trot watching the Posh.

Christine Malinowski Dear old Christine bless her she tells me she has supported the club for over fifty years and I am sure a regular traveller on the away travel coaches for thirty of them. She used to come with her Mum and when she passed away we all used to look after her on the away days still she fell ill and had part of her leg amputed and now lives in Residential Care with a lovely carer just round the corner from me in Fletton and always drop her a programme in for every away game he is still a regular at home in the Main Stand Disabled area. She still brings her little book to the games think see either writes down the scorers how they played or their phone numbers. One of the standing jokes we played on her was did she have her passport when we played in Wales but after a few journeys she got wise to that she misses her away trips and when I see her it's How many coaches going to away matches will you get me a progeham bless her. She has had many favourite players but Chris Turner was her favourite.

Joan or Joanie Hill One of the best looking young ladies I have met at London Road in her two spells at the club. Held several positions at the club including PA to her dear friend Barry Fry, player liaison officer and Community Officer very involved in setting up the Academy. Was a great loss to the club and the game in general as was held in very high regard by all who knew her? She left us on the 21st May after a long and brave fight against cancer and her funeral was quite rightly held at the Cathedral a fitting tribute on the actual day I retired from work the 12th June 2013. Can remember her Joanie challenge when we were running on Barry Fry's money the dressing room was so run down she asked local firms to either donate materials or to supply labour to update it I spend a fortnight of my annual holiday labouring in it and a plaque is now in the Main tunnel corridor to Joan's and the people involved in the challenge. As well as serving the Posh she served Cardiff City and Birmingham City. Only had a cross with her in jest about me calling the team over the air when working with Radio Cambridgeshire but they were rubbish at the time. At her funeral Barry Fry described her as the clubs unsung hero who had a heart as big as a Boeing 747 what a fitting tribute to a great lady.

Mark Tracey alias Ginge Think have know him for over twenty or more years the young lad who used to be the ball boy at the Training ground was adopted as the lucky mascot by team and appears prominently in the pictures at Wembley on the pitch with the 1991/2 team. He had many different roles at the club in the Youth set up and we worked together for a few seasons looking after Junior Posh activities at the Training Ground around the mid nineties at Alf Hands field at Eye playing games home and away at other team's junior clubs and running coaches to them. One of the nicest not so young men now you could meet always has a chat always about football and always has a grin of his face. Since leaving Posh has had roles in Youth set ups at Luton, South end and now is Chief Scout at rivals Cambridge United and can be seen at mid week Posh games and keeping an eye at our Reserve games. My Sharon will be pleased have wrote about him she loved him. Not a bad career for a man with two left feet blesses him.

Peter and Sandie Lane What they don't know about the Posh is not worth knowing Peter is the clubs historian and writes an article every game in the Posh programme like me has clocked up about sixty years of suffering and glory watching our beloved Posh. He is the curator of our Posh Hall of Fame which now has 28 members and a big waiting list the collection is now proudly positioned in the Main Reception at the ground. First meet him when he was playing local Peterborough Sunday League Football with the nickname rattler can't remember him being a prolific goals corer for his team called Borough United the mind boggles. Sandie tells me his Posh player of all time is Dennis Emery and she has two Tommy Robson in the early years of watching bet she stood at London Road he said he always jumped up the railings when he scored

## The Posh Affair 125

a goal near the best lady young lady Sandie was Miss Posh in 1977 and her more recent player was Craig Mackail-Smith. Used to see a lot of them both when Sharon was ill and opting to stay near to home with watching AFC Stamford where they were Commercial Managers for a few seasons. Tells me his one desertion from watching the Posh was going to watch the Panthers while the Posh were at home when Jim Iley was the boss.

Noel Luke Works with me on match days being a host in the hospitality areas he played 336 times for the club but only six good ones he tells me one of those was at Wembley against Stockport County. Served under Chris Turner but now know not to ask him to say a few words about him on the ground tour he is very reluctant to pass comment think they did not see eye to eye. He is quite modest that nobody paid money for him he was the original Bossman. Liked playing under Noel Cantwell said you could express yourself with him as manager. This likeable chap tells me he was only ever booked once in his career and that was for encroachment that says a lot about him. His picture stands proudly in the Hall of Fame.

Mick Jones Alias Mr Posh who recently was awarded a trophy from the FA for his 25 years in the role his predecessors being in the early days being Tom Keeble and Neville McAlpine can remember Jack Carmichael l doing it once and finishing up on his backside before retirement he could be found cleaning windows around the city centre and his much younger days as a singer mostly at the Halcyon now the Hungry Horse and local public houses as lead singer for the Big Four. Would think he is one of the longest serving mascots in the Football League and certainly the best dressed although he does not get as much attention and whistles as his glamorous match day granddaughter Miss Posh Jess Weaver. Asked who was his posh player of all time he went with Dennis Emery for the earlier years and Ken Charlery for the most recent. Now joined on match days with Peter Burrow sponsored by Forever Posh, PB from Princebuild who are my keepers at half time with the children's groups and Mick the Skip from Mick George who does so much for the local teams in the locality.

Gary Cooper People who remembers him will find this a strange choice a very wayward young man who was always in trouble if my memory serves me right he climbed over the Glebe Road wall and had an altercation with a supporter who was giving him some stick. He always had an eye for Sharon Anne and always got us tickets for the away games. Often used to bump into him in the city and him to ask me how I thought he was playing. After being so inspiring in the victory over Liverpool and in previous rounds he did a runner and missed out on the Wembley trip and a medal. Have asked Noel Luke does any of the team know where he is now or why he did a disappearing act. After leaving Posh he joined Birmingham City under the man who was brought so many good young players to the club or own Barry Fry when he left them he went into non league to not be heard of again although another Cooper Steve Zebedee scored to take us to Wembley.

Steve and Sam Downing Two people who do such a good job not only at the Posh but many other clubs in the Football League giving children with life threatening illnesses, bereaved children and disadvantage ones the chance to spend a day with their families at their favourite team with the charity Free Kicks. This has been in operation for over ten years and given over 750 children the chance. Steve has supported the club since 1974 a very famous year his best game seen was the play at Huddersfield in 1991/2 and his best player was George Boyd.

Sam best game was play offs at Old Trafford and favourite players Aaron McLean, George Boyd and Grant McCann

Ernie Balmer alias Geordie hailed from Shildon in County Durham where his father was a coal miner can't remember what brought his to this area but know he moved to the Spalding area working in the greenhouses and played lots of local football in that area one of his team mates was our own Bill Harvey. Was a regular on the coaches when I started going used to talk about trips to games well before my time and used to tell some good stories about his life to me and Sharon Anne who always sat beside him on the coach he was her adopted granddad on away days. A lovely old gent who gave us a few scares in his last years on the away travel never had a bad word to say about anybody. Sadly passed away late in 2000.

Nigel Cowling He like we has supported the club for 60 years his first game being the Cup game against Lincoln City way back in 1957 lived in the city till 1986 then moved to Sheffield asked David Ringham who was a director at the club then he did not get back to him and he was travelling away to every game since unless when we play the Blades. He went for Micky Halsall as best player for the club and most memorable game the Play off second leg against Huddersfield and does the programme exchange with Mick Sexton.

Tommy Henry Robson Have now perhaps worked at least over ten seasons or more with him at the ground with my ground tours for the sponsors etc and he being the host for the day. Don't really need to say much here all his career and his stories are well documented in my memories great servant to the club always has time for everybody who are oldies like me who remember him playing.

Alf Hand A lovely old gentlemen has been a director of the club he thinks over 50 years he used to have the training ground many years ago in his back garden in his farm at Eye I and spent many Saturday mornings down their when looking after Junior Posh with Marc Tracey alias Ginge like me and Anne lost his daughter Caroline very young in life at 36 in 2000 with Cystic Fibrosis for many years she was the clubs secretary and we have the Caroline Hand Executive Suite at the ground named after her. Alf was always accompanied by his lovely wife Pat in the boardroom and at games both home and away but sadly passed away four years ago such a lovely lady.

Mary Foxon The lady who always answers the phone at the club often takes the flax from supporters has been with the club for over 15 years and never seen a game at home as she has to man the office and the phones. She like me and Anne knows what it's like to lose a daughter she and her husband lost theirs suddenly with a stroke leaving a young family four years ago so we have a lot in common and often speak about it. She has watched Posh play away from home at Wembley etc and her favourite players are George Boyd, Arron McLeon and Craig Mackail-Smith as she did their contracts with them and she said they were lovely lads

Lenny Barletta One of our original hooligans could always be seen at away games organising his troops on his mobile hope he had a good contract. Has had several banning orders can remember seeing him on the sea front at Blackpool all huddled up and bumping into Steve Polland then our Police Liaison Officer bit like Dixon of Dock Green good afternoon Lenny what are you doing here and needless to say he did not get in. He tells me he did get in on banning order at Wembley for the Darlington game he had his face painted and wore a wig. He always knew were stood with me if he came on the coaches if you don't behave you never come again which he always respected. Supported the club over 30 years now mellowed and bring his nephew to games his best player for the club Ken Charley and best match Play off against Huddersfield. He always got the sharp end of Sharon Anne's tongue when he was a bad boy.

Rev. Richard Longfoot Our club vicar for 13 years did us the honour of taking Sharon Anne's funeral service like me he has a long affair with the club 64 years longer than me. His parents were supporters and took him along one of his early memories was watching us play and he remembered the actual date 19th November 1955 in a F.A. Cup 1st Round game against Ipswich Town the Posh winning 3-1 with goals from George Hair a brace and Dennis Emery with a gate of over 20,000 remembers being lifted over the wooden fence to pitch side so I could he could see better as he says you would not have that happen today.

With the number of years supported the club he went for Dennis Emery in the early years and in the modern era has gone for George Boyd his stand out game was the Second Leg play offs in 2011 against Milton Keynes.

Michael Wright A man who has made more appearances on the London Road pitch helping voluntary for 15 seasons than any players helping the grounds man with his match day duties and a folker on the pitch. Been a fan for 58 years he is a bit younger than me the game against Gillingham for the Championship in 1973/4 is his choice of the best game seen. His favourite player choice is keeper Tony Millington. Spent many matches shovelling snow off the pitch together remember one game still doing it when the players came out. His service was rewarded with a presentation at the end of this season by the club.

Peter Burrow alias Wayne Daley the man in the suit had two spells in the suit looked by all the kids a flipping nuisance to us adults with his antics we need some fun at the ground as it's like being in a library at many games. Peter Burrow spends time at all related initiatives including visiting local schools with players, parties etc in his outfit kindly sponsored by Forever Posh. Not in his good books at the minute kept calling him Wayne at the recent Easter Egg Hunt in front of the children. Best Posh game play off final win at Old Trafford against Huddersfield Town when he performed in his outfit favourite player was Jimmy Bullard who was as mad as him he told me.

I Think it apt as I end my book with pieces about supporters who can remember further back than me.

Ray Wright Tells me he has been working at the club mainly as a gateman for over sixty years he actually played for the club under Sam Haden remember him coaching us in the local Fletton Recreation Ground which now stands empty where have all the children gone on their X Boxes etc. Also played under Jack Fairbrother and George Swindon and was captain of the 'A' Team playing in the Peterborough League now aged 87 years young. His most favourite season being 1960-1, his favourite player was Billy Hails and best game seen beating the Arsenal in the FA Cup.

Ray served under also George Swindon and Jack Fairbrother, was captain of the Posh A team.

Jack Beeby Tells me he now in his eighties and still remember him on my early years travelling on the Shows coaches to away games. Always thought he met his wife June on the coaches but tells me that's not correct but it was when he worked on then British Rail and met her on a train coming back from watching the Posh at Crystal Palace so they did have something in common and travelled together away for many years. But now bless her has to listen to it on the radio and Jacks opinion when he gets home. Still one of the few shareholders at the club and always ready to ask questions at meetings about the club he loves. Very hard for him to pick his best players after seventy years of supporting the club he tells me his first game was against Desborough Town think it was in the FA Cup way back in 1954 like me he remembers the old days better and his best players at the club were Andy Donaldson and George Swindon. We have something in common we usually see the game the same if its rubbish we speak the truth.

I would like to Thank Joe Dent of Peterborough United
for the images in the book.

Also Peter and Sandie Lane for allowing me to use
the images from the Posh Hall of Fame.

Also to all the people players, managers and supporters like myself so many now sadly not with us for giving me so many memories and enabled me to put together *A Posh Affair* in Memory of our dear daughter SHARON ANNE EVANS. Who was a SPECIAL DAUGHTER, DEEP IN OUR HEARTS YOUR MEMORY IS KEPT. TO LOVE, TO CHERISH AND NEVER FORGET. GOD BLESS FROM MUM, DAD AND LADY PIP

xxx